T0328197

Cambridge Elements ≡

Elements in Magic
edited by
Marion Gibson
University of Exeter

CREATIVE HISTORIES OF WITCHCRAFT

France, 1790–1940

Poppy Corbett
Newcastle University

Anna Kisby Compton
Independent Scholar

William G. Pooley
University of Bristol

CAMBRIDGE
UNIVERSITY PRESS

CAMBRIDGE
UNIVERSITY PRESS

University Printing House, Cambridge CB2 8BS, United Kingdom

One Liberty Plaza, 20th Floor, New York, NY 10006, USA

477 Williamstown Road, Port Melbourne, VIC 3207, Australia

314–321, 3rd Floor, Plot 3, Splendor Forum, Jasola District Centre,
New Delhi – 110025, India

103 Penang Road, #05–06/07, Visioncrest Commercial, Singapore 238467

Cambridge University Press is part of the University of Cambridge.

It furthers the University's mission by disseminating knowledge in the pursuit of
education, learning, and research at the highest international levels of excellence.

www.cambridge.org
Information on this title: www.cambridge.org/9781009221030
DOI: 10.1017/9781009221054

© Poppy Corbett, Anna Kisby Compton, and William G. Pooley 2022

First published 2022

A catalogue record for this publication is available from the British Library.

ISBN 978-1-009-22103-0 Paperback
ISSN 2732-4087 (online)
ISSN 2732-4079 (print)

Creative Histories of Witchcraft

France, 1790–1940

Elements in Magic

DOI: 10.1017/9781009221054
First published online: May 2022

Poppy Corbett
Newcastle University

Anna Kisby Compton
Independent Scholar

William G. Pooley
University of Bristol

Author for correspondence: William G. Pooley, william.pooley@gmail.com

Abstract: How can researchers study magic without destroying its mystery? Drawing on a collaborative project between the playwright Poppy Corbett, the poet Anna Kisby Compton, and the historian William G. Pooley, this Element presents thirteen tools for creative-academic research into magic, illustrated through case studies from France (1790–1940) and examples from creative outputs: write to discover; borrow forms; use the whole page; play with footnotes; erase the sources; write short; accumulate fragments; re-enact; improvise; use dialogue; change perspective; make methods of metaphors; use props. These tools are ways to 'untell' the dominant narratives that shape stereotypes of the 'witch' which frame belief in witchcraft as ignorant and outdated. Writing differently suggests ways to think and feel differently, to stay with the magic rather than explaining it away. The Element includes practical creative exercises to try as well as research materials from French newspaper and trial sources from the period.

Keywords: Creative histories, witchcraft, French history, writing as research, practice-based research

ISBNs: 9781009221030 (PB), 9781009221054 (OC)
ISSNs: 2732-4087 (online), 2732-4079 (print)

Contents

1 Introduction

A writer's real work is the endless winnowing of sentences,

The relentless exploration of possibilities,

The effort, over and over again, to see in what you started out to say

The possibility of something that you didn't know you could.[1]

All too often a sense of magic is lost in the process of studying magic.[2]

1.1 History, Magic, Creativity

This Element is a call to arms for historians to embrace creative research methods and alternative ways of presenting histories. 'Practice-based research' is now a well-established methodology in many arts disciplines and social sciences. Textbooks explore how and when to use creative practices and how to address the risks and shortcomings of practice-based research.[3] But historians have generally been slower to take up the idea of creative research methods, and there are very few examples of how-to guides that others can draw on.[4] This Element is a case study in what creative practice can do for historians and other humanities researchers. How might the methods of dramatists, poets, and other artists help historians understand a topic like magic?

Academic research into histories of magic struggles to capture the mystery at the heart of supernatural experiences and beliefs. We can blame our sources, which are often hostile to magical beliefs, whether they treat them as heresies or superstitions. Such hostile sources distort the histories we write, encouraging historians to tell the same stories of 'secularization' in the modern period and to treat magic like outsiders. Yet, as Chris Gosden has noted in an ambitious survey of magic across all of human history, 'rumours of the death of magic have been constantly exaggerated'.[5] Historians have long known that this 'decline of magic' may fit with a general pattern in elite attitudes but makes

---

[1] Verlyn Klinkenborg, *Several Short Sentences about Writing* (New York: Vintage Books, 2013), 14.

[2] Owen Davies, *Magic: A Very Short Introduction* (Oxford: Oxford University Press, 2012), 112.

[3] See, for example, Helen Kara, *Creative Research Methods in the Social Sciences* (Bristol: Policy Press, 2015).

[4] Although see Robert Bickers, Tim Cole, Marianna Dudley, et al. 'Creative Dislocation: An Experiment in Collaborative Historical Research', *History Workshop Journal* 90:1 (2020), 273–96; Hillary Davidson, 'The Embodied Turn: Making and Remaking Dress as an Academic Practice', *Fashion Theory* 23:3 (2019), 329–62.

[5] Chris Gosden, *The History of Magic: From Alchemy to Witchcraft, from the Ice Age to the Present* (London: Viking, 2020). The same year that Gosden wrote this, Michael Hunter published an updated account of this process of disenchantment in Britain: *The Decline of Magic: Britain in the Enlightenment* (New Haven, CT: Yale University Press, 2020).

less sense among the broader populations of modern Europe.[6] Historians of popular magic have learned to read against the grain in order to uncover submerged perspectives about magic in hostile sources.[7] The methods of imagination and speculation they have used to do this have tended to come from anthropology or psychoanalysis.[8]

This Element explores a different set of imaginative techniques to address the fundamental challenge of understanding magic in the past: creative practices, including poetry, drama, and other forms of creative writing. The Element draws on the collaborative project 'Creative Histories of Witchcraft: France, 1790–1940', which brought together a poet (Anna Kisby Compton), a playwright (Poppy Corbett), and a historian (Will Pooley) to explore cases of witchcraft from across this long period. In what follows, we explain our project and how we did it, providing hands-on exercises for other researchers, creative practitioners, and teachers to try out for themselves.

1.2 Witchcraft in France, 1790–1940

The work for this Element began with Will's research into witchcraft in France between 1790 and 1940.[9] Although historians tend to think of witchcraft more as an early modern problem than one from the nineteenth century, specialists have long known that witchcraft beliefs did not wither with the end of the officially sanctioned witch trials in Europe in the seventeenth and eighteenth centuries.[10] Despite effectively decriminalizing witchcraft relatively early – in 1684 – French courts have continued to deal with questions of harmful magic up

---

[6] See the pioneering work on British supernatural beliefs by Owen Davies, *Witchcraft, Magic, and Culture, 1736–1951* (Manchester: Manchester University Press, 1999).

[7] A much-debated example was provided by Carlo Ginzburg's *The Night Battles: Witchcraft and Agrarian Cults in the Sixteenth and Seventeenth Centuries*, trans. Anne Tedeschi and John Tedeschi (London: Routledge and Kegan Paul, 1983).

[8] Lyndal Roper, *Oedipus and the Devil: Witchcraft, Sexuality, and Religion in Early Modern Europe* (New York and London: Routledge, 1994); Diane Purkiss, *The Witch in History: Early Modern and Twentieth-Century Representations* (New York and London: Routledge, 1996).

[9] This research draws on Ronald Hutton's definition of the witch as a human being believed to cause supernatural harm, usually to people within their own community. See Ronald Hutton, 'Anthropological and Historical Approaches to Witchcraft: Potential for a New Collaboration?' *The Historical Journal* 47:2 (2004), 413–34, 421–3.

[10] Some countries did not actually repeal anti-witchcraft legislation until the nineteenth century. See, for instance, the Irish case discussed in Andrew Sneddon and John Fulton, 'Witchcraft, the Press, and Crime in Ireland, 1822-1922', *The Historical Journal* 62:3 (2019), 741–64. For overviews of witchcraft after the witch trials, see Willem de Blécourt and Owen Davies (eds.), *Witchcraft Continued: Popular Magic in Modern Europe* (Manchester: Manchester University Press, 2004); Bengt Ankarloo and Stuart Clark (eds.), *Witchcraft and Magic in Europe: The Eighteenth and Nineteenth Centuries* (Philadelphia: University of Pennsylvania Press, 1999).

to the present day.[11] Between 1790 and 1940, there were close to 1,000 different cases either tried in regional courts or described in the national and local press.

Why were the authorities interested in witchcraft if witchcraft itself was not a crime in this period? The answer can be found with other types of crime whose origins lie with witchcraft, such as some types of fraud. Around two thirds of the cases identified from newspapers and judicial sources involved accusations of fraud or of practising medicine without a licence. These prosecutions were not normally launched against suspected 'witches' themselves. Instead, they targeted the 'unwitchers' who took payment to help deal with spells and curses. Since the courts did not believe in magic, taking payment for these services constituted an obvious fraud, not to mention a contravention of the rules on medical practice if the suspected witchcraft involved an illness.

The other category of crime that covered a large number of the cases was violence against persons. Around a quarter of the cases are what Owen Davies has called 'reverse witch trials': prosecutions brought against people who abused – whether physically or verbally – people that they accused of being witches.[12] The remaining cases include rare attempts to prosecute witches for witchcraft, as well as retaliations by men and women accused of being witches, crimes of nuisance, vagrancy, and some rare sexual offences where ideas about witchcraft were muddled into legal prosecutions and police investigations.

These cases present modern historians with many of the same challenges and opportunities that the cases from the famous witch trials presented to early modern historians. They seem to offer unrivalled access into the often-unspoken assumptions around gender, sexuality, and the family.[13] They are like strange windows into the subjectivity of people in the past.[14] Yet so much of what historians want to say about the cases must remain speculative and imaginative. The sources are filled with silences, contradictions, and material that makes no

---

[11] For the eighteenth century, see Ulrike Krampl, *Les secrets des faux sorciers: Police, magie et escroquerie à Paris au XVIIIe siècle* (Paris: EHESS, 2012). The best survey of the modern period remains: Owen Davies, 'Witchcraft Accusations in France, 1850-1990', in Willem de Blécourt and Owen Davies (eds.), *Witchcraft Continued: Popular Magic in Modern Europe* (Manchester: Manchester University Press, 2004). Anthropologists including Marcelle Bouteiller and Jeanne Favret-Saada documented witchcraft beliefs firsthand during the 1950s-1970s. See Marcelle Bouteiller, *Sorciers et jeteurs de sorts* (Paris: Plon, 1958) and Jeanne Favret-Saada, *Deadly Words: Witchcraft in the Bocage*, trans. Catherine Cullen (Cambridge: Cambridge University Press, 1980).

[12] See Owen Davies, 'Researching Reverse Witch Trials in Nineteenth- and Early Twentieth-Century England', in Jonathan Barry, Owen Davies, and Cornelie Usborne (eds.), *Cultures of Witchcraft from the Middle Ages to the Present: Essays in Honour of Willem de Blécourt* (Cham: Palgrave Macmillan, 2018), 215–33.

[13] This is the argument in Tessie Liu, 'Le Patrimoine Magique: Reassessing the Power of Women in Peasant Households in Nineteenth-Century France', *Gender and History* 6:1 (1994), 13–36.

[14] See, for instance, Roper, *Oedipus and the Devil*.

sense to readers today. And, like all historians of witchcraft, historians of more recent European witchcraft struggle to convey the variety and complexity of witchcraft phenomena in the face of powerful popular cultural stereotypes of the 'witch' today.[15]

But the history of witchcraft after the witch trials also presents different challenges and opportunities to the better-known topic of the early modern trials. Modern witchcraft is chronologically awkward. The folklorists and some early historians thought of witchcraft as a 'survival'.[16] More recent work has tended to emphasize the constant adaptations and mutations of witchcraft belief. Inspired by anthropologists, historians can now explore the psychological and economic 'modernity' of modern European witchcraft.[17] Many people from the same generations that lived through the emergence of dynamic psychology, the Pasteurian revolution, and the First World War also believed in witches.

Also, there are major differences in the institutional frameworks that governed the early modern and the modern cases. When it came to witchcraft, both the Church and the legal system changed beyond recognition. Not only had ecclesiastical support for prosecutions largely evaporated, but the legal system had almost no interest in witchcraft itself as a criminal problem. With the evaporation of this institutional focus, the 'witches' themselves also disappeared. Where the early modern trials produced a discourse of witchcraft with at least two sides – that of the victims, and that of the witches' confessions, extracted under duress, if not torture – the modern period, Thomas Waters has pointed out, is characterized by witchcraft largely 'without witches'.[18] Meanwhile, other contexts became increasingly important for criminal justice and witchcraft, such as France's status as a colonial power and the issues of race, justice, and culture that came with maintaining overseas territories.[19]

Nor do these cases of modern witchcraft necessarily conform to the patterns that historians might expect, based on the dismissive attitudes of newspaper editors or the romantic nostalgia of the folklorists. Many cases took place in urban settings, such as Lyon, Marseille, and Rouen. Paris itself – much to the dismay of contemporaries – was a hotspot of witchcraft disputes in the

---

[15] A key point in Purkiss, *The Witch in History*.

[16] Among the historians, see, for instance, Judith Devlin *The Superstitious Mind: French Peasants and the Supernatural in the Nineteenth Century* (New Haven, CT: Yale University Press, 1987).

[17] For example, see Thomas Waters *Cursed Britain: A History of Witchcraft and Black Magic in Modern Times* (New Haven, CT: Yale University Press, 2019). For a key inspiration, see Peter Geschiere, *The Modernity of Witchcraft: Politics and the Occult in Postcolonial Africa* (Charlottesville: University Press of Virginia, 1997).

[18] Waters, *Cursed Britain*, 257.

[19] See Aaron Freundschuh, *The Courtesan and the Gigolo: The Murders in the Rue Montaigne and the Dark Side of Empire in Nineteenth-century Paris* (Stanford, CA: Stanford University Press, 2017).

nineteenth century.[20] Perhaps even more surprisingly for what historians know about early modern witchcraft, the information available from these cases suggests that the majority (fifty-seven per cent) of the people feared as 'witches' in this period were men.[21]

It is in order to puncture such easy assumptions about magic in modernity that we propose a turn to creative methods.

1.3 The Need for Creative Histories of Magic

The need for creative histories of magic is part of a wider turn to 'creative histories', 'an umbrella term for diverse traditions and genealogies of scholarship, such as the imaginative, the fictional, and the genre-challenging'.[22] Saidiya Hartman, for instance, has written of the need for speculation, imagination, and amplification in her 'serial biography of a generation' of young black girls at the start of the twentieth century. Her writing draws on archival research but also openly speculates and embroiders, blurring the lines that many historians would draw between factual research and fiction.[23] Similarly, Matt Houlbrook's work on the confidence trickster Netley Lucas blends research with creative forms of presentation, such as a television script or a letter to his research subject.[24] As Sarah Knott has argued, different histories invite different forms and conventions. Her own work on mothering is written in fragments which focus on verbs, because of the fragmentation characteristic of early motherhood, and her desire to emphasize mothering as an activity performed by a range of actors, rather than a fixed identity.[25] Hartman, Houlbrook, and Knott's books show how much interest there is in creative historical writing, but researchers and students who want to follow their lead will struggle to find examples of writing manuals for creative historians. In what follows, we describe the methods we have found most useful for exploring histories of magic and provide hands-on exercises to try. If creative historical work is as much about process as output – as one group of historians has put it – there is a pressing need for examples that model process, rather than just presenting creative outputs.[26]

---

[20] William G. Pooley, 'Magical Capital: Witchcraft and the Press in Paris, c.1789-1939', in Karl Bell (ed.), *Supernatural Cities: Enchantment, Anxiety and Spectrality* (Woodbridge, Suffolk: Boydell Press, 2019), 25–44.

[21] This is based on the gender – where known – of 578 suspected witches from 997 cases. Of these, 247 were women and 331 were men.

[22] Bickers et al., 'Creative Dislocation', 274.

[23] Saidiya Hartman, *Wayward Lives, Beautiful Experiments: Intimate Histories of Riotous Black Girls, Troublesome Women, and Queer Radicals* (New York: W.W. Norton, 2019).

[24] Matt Houlbrook, *Prince of Tricksters: The Incredible True Story of Netley Lucas, Gentleman Crook* (Chicago, IL: University of Chicago Press, 2016).

[25] Sarah Knott, *Mother: An Unconventional History* (London: Penguin, 2019).

[26] See Bickers et al., 'Creative Dislocation'.

These exercises draw on another set of traditions of creative historical work that have sometimes overlapped with, but often developed independently of, academic researchers: artist practitioners and community histories. Openstorytellers, for instance, are a company of performers with learning disabilities who have engaged with histories of disability by devising theatre pieces, such as their play about Fanny Fust, an eighteenth-century heiress with learning difficulties. Working on a performance in this way has allowed the members of the group to engage with histories that they could not access in other ways.[27] In a similar way, the artist Ruth Singer has described how making quilts was a way to bring all of the female criminals she researched 'together in one place and to remember them as real women not just as criminal statistics or a mugshot without a story'.[28] Beyond academic creative writing, a range of practitioners have explored ways to do history through visual arts, performance, re-enactment, and music. We need these creative methods because they allow us to take magic seriously, to go beyond easy stereotypes, and to appeal to different audiences.

Academic researchers are caught between two extremes when it comes to studying the history of magic. On the one hand, as both Stuart Clark and Diane Purkiss have pointed out, researchers struggle to accept that people really believed in the supernatural experiences they described. It has been easier for historians to accept that witchcraft was 'really' about gender or social tensions between rich and poor than to take the fear of witches seriously in its own right. As Purkiss puts it, historians' explanations have a tendency to explain too well, 'explaining witch-beliefs *away*'.[29] At the other extreme, researchers have arguably been too willing to believe that people in the past fervently believed in magic. Bruno Latour has called this a singularly 'modern' attitude to belief. 'A Modern', he points out, 'is someone who believes that others believe'.[30] Moderns think for themselves, unlike 'primitives' and 'pre-moderns', who naively and uniformly believe in magic, witchcraft, and other supernatural phenomena. The image of 'belief' that underpins this attitude to the academic study of magic, as Nils Bubandt has pointed out, does not fit well with the uncertainty and vagueness that characterizes witchcraft belief. Based on his

---

[27] The Company of Openstorytellers, Nicola Grove, Simon Jarrett, et al., 'The Fortunes and Misfortunes of Fanny Fust', in Andrew W. M. Smith (ed.), *Paper Trails: The Social Life of Archives and Collections* (London: UCL Press, forthcoming).

[28] Ruth Singer, *Criminal Quilts: Textiles Inspired by the Stories of Women Photographed in Stafford Prison 1877–1916* (Leicester: Independent Publishing Network, 2018), 19.

[29] Purkiss, *The Witch in History*, 60–5, 61. Stuart Clark, *Thinking with Demons: The Idea of Witchcraft in Early Modern Europe* (Oxford: Oxford University Press, 1997).

[30] Bruno Latour, *On the Modern Cult of the Factish Gods* (Durham, NC: Duke University Press, 2010), 2.

Indonesian fieldwork, Bubandt argues that witchcraft is more like a persistent doubt than a positive belief.[31]

Creative practices offer solutions both to the tendency to explain magic away and the tendency to depict belief as homogenous and absolute. Written forms and performance techniques drawn from poetry and theatre are a way to stay with the magic. As the poet Rebecca Tamás has written:

> Poetry, like the occult, embraces the necessary irrationality that exists squashed up against rationality in the material world. It does not 'reject' the rational, but it does extract what else is there, the elements that don't fit.[32]

Where academic research often follows conventions that encourage seamless, comprehensive, and definitive arguments, creative practices do not have to be directed towards firm conclusions. Instead, they preserve silences, speak in metaphors, juxtapose, hint, elaborate, or embroider in ways that are particularly valuable when trying to preserve the mysteries of magical experiences. Where academic conventions demand clearly articulated epistemologies, working through poetry or drama can be a way to defer truth claims and final interpretations, to leave some aspects of magic unresolved. The many different voices that speak through plays or poems allow multiple epistemologies to bump up against one another. The poet does not have to settle, nor does the playwright summarize her conclusions.

1.4 Format of the Element

This is a hands-on text. We have divided the Element into four thematic sections, which include thirteen specific tools for creative research into magic. These tools would also be a good starting point for teaching creative historical research methods. Like other creative non-fiction writers, we are less interested in outright invention than ways of re-using the past, histories that are 'creative, not falsified'.[33]

In search of historical 'fidelity', the second Section encourages researchers to:

1. Write to discover
2. Borrow other forms
3. Use the whole page
4. Play with footnotes

---

[31] Nils Bubandt, *The Empty Seashell: Witchcraft and Doubt on an Indonesian Island* (Ithaca, NY and London: Cornell University Press, 2014).

[32] Rebecca Tamás, 'Songs of Hecate', *The White Review*, 24 (2019), https://bit.ly/3tKjQV6.

[33] Gay Talese, 'Delving into Private Lives', in Mark Kramer and Wendy Call (eds.), *Telling True Stories: A Nonfiction Writer's Guide from the Nieman Foundation at Harvard University* (New York: Plume, 2007), 6–9, 7.

The third Section addresses the values of 'brevity', suggesting that researchers should:

5. Erase the sources
6. Write short
7. Accumulate fragments

The fourth Section turns to ideas of 'performance', inviting researchers to:

8. Re-enact
9. Improvise
10. Use dialogue

The fifth Section suggests tools for creative empathy:

11. Change perspective
12. Make methods of metaphors
13. Use props

Each section presents two case studies in detail, including cases of murder and infanticide, as well as minor mysteries without neat resolutions: a family whose animals mysteriously died or a couple of greengrocers who complained of a bewitched cupboard. In the epilogue, we reflect on these cases and on the processes involved in the thirteen creative tools we have suggested for researching magic.

The Element is written using some unusual layouts, forms, and genres. This style represents the fusion of our different styles of writing and viewpoints. Eclectic forms achieve eclectic aims. They listen to silences, represent multitude, and speak for the dead. There are moments where we describe some of our historical research and the individual cases we encountered on the project. Some of it is written poetically, in abstraction, dramatically, and in ways that will appear unfamiliar to historical researchers. But all of the Element explores the fundamental question of what happens when we bring creative and historical forms of writing together.

Different readers may want to use the Element in different ways. We do not assume any specialist knowledge of French history or the history of modern witchcraft, but instead propose methods and techniques for writing and researching. Creative practitioners may be familiar with many of these techniques but are likely to be less familiar with discussions of how they might be used for history. We discuss the value and purpose of these applications in the second half of this introduction and throughout the Element. Some sections will be of more interest to historians, such as the discussion of the creative turn in history. The sections can be used as standalone resources for working with students, researchers, or creative practitioners, although they contribute to an overall argument about creative practice as historical research. Readers in search of spells will find some, although mostly in fragmentary form. Like a dictionary or a technical manual, the Element is best enjoyed by dipping in and out in search of what you need.

As a three-way partnership between a playwright, a poet, and a historian, this Element straddles academic and practitioner interests. It departs from well-established models of 'historical advisors' or consultants who provide expertise for theatre companies and film productions, or professional artists who produce 'impact' work for academic researchers. What happens, instead, when research and creative practice work in equal partnership? We are less interested in art 'inspired' by history than art challenged by and developed in conversation with historical research.

We speak in many voices, reflecting the many different people who have collaborated and contributed to this work. We do provide references in footnotes and there is a list of references. Its eclecticism is a source of joy to us, but we could not approach the topic of witchcraft, even in this limited place and period, from every angle. Poppy, Anna, and Will brainstormed ideas, recording them on whiteboards, paper, and online documents. We dictated words to one another to write. We edited each other's writing, adding and trimming, rearranging and repurposing. We interviewed each other. We wrote each other letters. We translated words from one language to another and from one form to another. We took scripts and made them poems. We took sources and made them scripts. The format of the Element reflects these methods.

Others speak, too, because we wrote with others in ever-widening circles of conversation and adaptation. Some we interacted with in person. We would like to mention Ellie Chadwick, who produced and directed a rehearsed reading based on the project, and the actors Alan Coveney, Esme Patey-Ford, Joanna Cross, Matthew Bulgo, and Tobias Weatherburn. Nicola Burnett-Smith composed and performed original music for the rehearsed reading, in addition to appearing as part of the cast. We also worked with Shelley, Richard, Rebecca, and other members of the Bristol Open Circle Moot to discuss the meaning of magic to modern pagans. The poets Karen Dennison, Hilary Dyer, Lindsay Macgregor, E. E. Nobbs, Lydia Harris, and Caroline Davies collaborated with Anna as guest poets on the project, producing one long collaborative poem and a range of shorter individual pieces.[34]

---

[34] See https://creativewitchcraft.wordpress.com/guest-poets/

And the dead? Throughout the project we have been drawn to specific individuals whose lives we wanted to understand. In the words of the historical novelist Hilary Mantel:

> In imagination, we chase the dead, shouting, 'come back!' We may suspect that the voices we hear are an echo of our own, and the movement we see is our own shadow. But we sense the dead have a vital force still – they have something to tell us, something we need to understand.[35]

Some researchers will be more comfortable with a sense of mysterious connection to the past, and even supernatural communication across time.[36] Others may object that speculative, imagined, and improvised work of this kind lacks rigour. But a third approach is also possible: reserving judgement about the significance of practice-based or creative insights. Perhaps they open new questions. Perhaps they provide provocations that challenge the established facts. The final outputs from work like this do not necessarily capture its experiential significance, especially when these outputs are – like this Element – textual. There are ways of knowing that only come through doing. Sometimes the findings are new questions.

2 Fidelity

How does one write a history of the impossible?[37]
Tell all the truth but tell it slant –[38]

2.1 The Problem

What does it mean to write histories that are creative, yet accurate? This is a particularly pressing problem for histories of magic. Notoriously hard to define, 'magic' is a fluid category which can encompass everything from the fundamental rules of everyday life in cultures such as ancient Egypt to a special category of events and practices that somehow stand outside the normal way things work, as in post-Enlightenment European cultures.[39] It is a realm that few historians would openly profess to believe in. Marion Gibson has posed this

---

[35] Hilary Mantel, 'The Day is for the Living', *The Reith Lectures*, 2017. https://bit.ly/3Ixgau6.
[36] Carlo Ginzburg, for instance, has written of the 'nucleus of truth' in his 'absurd fantasizing' 'that [a historical] document was there waiting for me, and that my entire past life had predisposed me to find it'. *Threads and Traces: True, False, Fictive* (Berkeley: University of California Press, 2010), 222.
[37] Michel-Rolph Trouillot, *Silencing the Past: Power and the Production of History* (Boston, MA: Beacon Press, 1995), 73.
[38] Emily Dickinson, 'Tell All the Truth But Tell It Slant' [1951]. https://bit.ly/36jZby1.
[39] For one recent attempt to define magic, and an overview of Egyptian beliefs, see Gosden, *The History of Magic*, 1–2, 92–108.

problem as a question about how researchers decide what really happened: 'How … can one define a truthful story about this impossible crime?'[40] This ambiguous epistemological status makes witchcraft and other forms of magic paradigm cases for a broader problem that faces all historians: the problem of historical accuracy, reality, or truth, the quest to understand – in Leopold von Ranke's famous formulation – 'how things actually were'.[41]

Do truthful histories of witchcraft involve applying our own 'naturalistic' interpretation of what 'really' happened to the strange and fragmented stories that historical subjects told?[42] Or are accounts of historical beliefs that try to understand what people at the time really believed was happening in some senses closer to the texture of the past as it 'actually' was?[43] In this section, we argue for epistemological pluralism and open-mindedness. Everything historians and anthropologists know about supernatural beliefs such as witchcraft suggests that belief is highly contextual, variable, and shifting. Can our histories be as multivocal and undecided?

Working with theatrical and poetic techniques is a way to reject the absolutism of historiographical debates about truth and to instead refocus discussions on what we have termed 'fidelity'. Making use of his experience of writing plays drawing on LGBTQ histories, the playwright Stephen Hornby argues for replacing 'historical accuracy' with the idea of 'historical literacy'. For Hornby, this is a way to recognize the importance of 'creative choices' and even 'deliberate distortions' when producing plays grappling with the silences and inaccuracies of the archive.[44] No historical fact is innocent. As Michel-Rolph Trouillot has put it: 'The naming of the "fact" is itself a narrative of power disguised as innocence.'[45] How can historians come to terms with this in their writing? How can they, in the words of Natalie Zemon Davis, aspire not to 'proofs' but to 'historical possibilities'?[46]

One way is to learn from how creative writers such as Hornby think about fidelity to the past. Historians can think of their sources as 'found materials'.

---

[40] Marion Gibson, *Reading Witchcraft: Stories of Early English Witches* (London and New York: Routledge, 1999), 5.

[41] Leopold von Ranke, 'Preface: Histories of Romance and Germanic Peoples', in Fritz Stern (ed.), *The Varieties of History: From Voltaire to the Present* (London: Macmillan, 1970), 57.

[42] For a particularly bold example, see Edward Bever, *The Realities of Witchcraft and Popular Magic in Early Modern Europe: Culture, Cognition and Everyday Life* (London: Palgrave, 2008).

[43] An approach championed by Stuart Clark. See *Thinking with Demons*.

[44] Stephen Hornby, '"Stand Up if You're Gay!" *The Burnley Buggers' Ball*: The Dilemmas of Dramatizing Political History', Staging History Symposium, 26 April 2019, Bristol.

[45] Trouillot, *Silencing the Past*, 114.

[46] Natalie Zemon Davis, *A Passion for History: Conversations with Denis Crouzet* (Kirksville, MO: Truman State University Press, 2010), 22.

Rather than seeing writing as just the final stage of translating research into an output, they can see writing itself as a process of discovery. Using other forms can be a way to preserve the uncertainties and multivocality of historical magic. And we can bend our existing forms to new purposes by using the whole page and by playing with footnotes. We explore these techniques through the example of a murder case from 1886.

2.2 Case Study 1: Pouilloux, 1886

Shortly after lunch on 28 April 1886, Joseph Auloy shot his neighbour, Jacques Martin, twice with a revolver as the two men were walking back to the pottery factory where they worked.[47] Jacques Martin staggered away from the scene and made it back to the village, where he managed to give his side of the story before he bled to death. Joseph Auloy calmly continued back to work as if nothing had happened. A short time later, news reached the factory and his co-workers wrestled him into a shed to wait for the police.

From the moment that the murder investigation began, it was a struggle to establish the most basic facts about what had happened. The murderer's account of an unprovoked attack, forcing him to use his gun in self-defence, was at odds with what the victim had described before he died. Jacques Martin claimed that, far from attacking Auloy, it had been the murderer who started shouting at him, before suddenly pulling a gun and shooting him. Auloy had an obvious motive for dishonesty: if he could persuade the investigation and later a jury that he had acted in self-defence, he would face a much lighter sentence. But Auloy's story also suffered from another major inconsistency. According to a range of local witnesses, in the lead-up to the murder both the murderer and his wife, Claudine, had come to suspect Jacques Martin of bewitching their household. And Auloy made no secret of his suspicions, telling other people from the village that he was planning to 'take on' his tormentors, the witches. Yet when this was put to the murderer, he flatly denied it, ridiculing the belief in witches.

This apparent change of opinion frustrated the investigators and convinced the court-appointed medical expert that the murderer and his wife were an example of shared psychosis, or *folie à deux*. According to the doctor's theory, Claudine exhibited clear delusions. She thought that a range of everyday phenomena, such as rubbish in their yard, strange smells, and unusual sensations, were caused by unnamed witches. The doctor believed that the relationship between the man and wife was so close and intense that she then transmitted her delusions to the murderer. This is how the doctor could explain

---

[47] See Archives départementales de l'Aube, 2 U 738, and *Le Courrier de Saône-et-Loire*, 31 October 1886.

the murderer's change of stance: once he was arrested and separated from her, Joseph Auloy stopped believing in witches.

What can we do with this story? Or rather, how do we deal with the multiplicity of stories that the murderer, his wife, the victim, other witnesses, and the psychiatrist told about what happened? How can poetic and theatrical writing help to analyse and represent what might have happened?

2.3 Write to Discover

Historians are accustomed to thinking of writing as the final stage of the research process. What happens when we begin with it, when we make writing one of the first ways we engage with our sources? Writing, as the sociologist Laurel Richardson has emphasized, is 'a method of inquiry'. Elizabeth Adams St Pierre describes her own experiences of writing to discover:

> *Thought happened in the writing.* As I wrote, I watched word after word appear on the computer screen – ideas, theories, I had not thought before I wrote them. Sometimes I wrote something so marvellous it startled me. *I doubt I could have had such a thought by thinking alone.*[48]

Writing does not have to commit us to one version of events or another. It can be something like the anthropologist's method of 'thick description', popularized by Clifford Geertz.[49] Free-writing around a primary source, like thick description, works to capture as much fine-detailed information as possible. It asks that we get the thing right before we get it interpreted.

But perhaps more than an anthropological technique, this is a creative one. Historians can treat their sources in similar ways to how poets work with 'found materials'. Or they can employ the techniques of 'documentary' or 'verbatim' theatre, which reproduce recorded speech.[50] Towards the end of a year working on these materials with a historian, Anna reflected on what she felt other historians could learn from this kind of creative use of historical documents:

> They need to slow down. From what you've said, Will, historians are often skim reading, and you don't have that time to sit with a source.

---

[48] Laurel Richardson and Elizabeth Adams St Pierre, 'Writing: A Method of Inquiry', in Norman Denzin and Yvonna Lincoln (eds.), *Handbook of Qualitative Research* (London: Sage, 2000), 818–38, 826 (emphasis in original).

[49] Clifford Geertz, *The Interpretation of Cultures: Selected Essays* (New York: Basic Books, 2000), 3–30.

[50] See, for instance, Will Hammond and Dan Steward, *Verbatim, Verbatim: Contemporary Documentary Theatre* (London: Oberon, 2012); Janelle Reinelt, 'The Promise of Documentary', in Alison Forsyth and Chris Megson (eds.), *Get Real. Performance Interventions* (London: Palgrave Macmillan, 2009).

We worked over and over translations of the deposition documents in the
Pouilloux case, following the advice of the poet Ted Hughes:

> Do not think it up laboriously, as if you were working out mental arithmetic.
> Just look at it, touch it, smell it, listen to it, turn yourself into it. When you do
> this, the words look after themselves, like magic.[51]

Instead of trying to work out what 'really' happened, Anna wrote poems that
recover and condense the baffling feelings Claudine blamed on witchcraft.
There are no factual inventions or additions in Anna's poem 'The Murderer's
Wife':

> It's true when he was drunk he took easy offence.
> In his nightshirt, he chased a neighbour with an axe.
>
> No-one was hurt. Yes, we built a fence. Any excuse
> and they would tramp our yard, let my chickens loose.
> It weighed on him. Our boundaries were ours to guard.
>
> Hear this – a list of things they tossed into our yard:
> skin of toad, rocks, bones criss-cross like embers to touch.
>
> No, we don't attend the village church. Bullets may
> fend off wild beasts. Tell me, what's the meaning of this:
>
> on my doorstep, inside its broken shell, a stillborn chick.
> It's true he was quick to offence when he was drunk
>
> and he would list aloud the things they threw into our yard.
> My husband listened hard as I described the gob of spittle
> hawked at my bucket as I dipped it in the well.
>
> Judge me as you will. A murderer's wife is a victim, delusional
> or false. I sweep up whispers. The doctor walks on eggshells.

As a first step, poetic writing becomes a form of noticing, of giving weight to
material objects, and emphasizing the uncertainty and disagreement that char-
acterize the primary sources. Anna described her aims in writing poems from
Claudine's point of view:

> I wanted to put the reader close to Claudine, whom I felt was scapegoated
> within the historical records as well as, possibly, within her community. But
> also, I knew her voice had to be changeable – firstly, because the archive
> sources demonstrate how many versions of Claudine there are, how slippery
> are the facts, and secondly, to demonstrate how I, the writer, am implicated in
> her voice, never getting it 'right'. I wrote several poems from different angles
> to convey this 'versionality'.

---

[51] Ted Hughes, *Poetry in the Making: A Handbook for Writing* (London: Faber, 1969), 18.

This form of writing as noticing is also a way to shake ourselves out of a false sense of familiarity with 'witchcraft'. After working with these techniques of writing as noticing, Poppy reflected:

> This has demolished my preconceptions about witchcraft. The topic covers so much more than I imagined it would when we started.

Instead of the deep-seated stereotypes of 'the witch' that have sedimented in popular cultures over the last 500 years, Anna's poem 'The Five Delusions of Claudine A' takes the reader close to the feeling of bewitchment:

> *(i) taste*
> Water has the flavour of blood.
> Try swallowing a toad stuck with pins. A clot.
> Clear your throat. A neighbour spat in the well.
>
> *(ii) sight*
> Try using your vulture-sharp eyes. Whose bones
> are these arranged on my plate in cruciform?
> His sidelong glance casts a spell.
>
> *(iii) touch*
> Bowls are frogs leaping from my grasp.
> Try binding your hands with hangman's rope.
> Stoop. Bear broken pots that burn like hell.
>
> *(iv) smell*
> I make a bonfire of my dress. It smokes
> like dung cakes. Eggs turn. Try breathing in
> sulphur, a bitch in heat. My house is my cell.
>
> *(v) sound*
> Whispers make love like fleas.
> I've *Hail Marys* coming out of my ears, drownings
> of gossip. Try listening. Tell. Don't tell.

Anna's poems are what she calls 'a synthesis of imaginative leaps':

> Claudine's own words sourced from police records, background reading on women's domestic work [e.g. in Segalen's Love and Power[52]], and what I've learnt about the objects of witchcraft used for laying curses. Reading these poems during a meeting with a modern pagan group, I noticed how the intimate voice provoked identification with Claudine. I could feel the distance between past and present collapsing as the group discussed her motives and feelings. I then watched the group's sympathies leap beyond the version of

---

[52] Martine Segalen, *Love and Power in the Peasant Family: Rural France in the Nineteenth Century*, trans. Sarah Matthews (London: Blackwell, 1983).

Claudine presented in the poem – for example, discussion took in the character and feelings of Claudine's husband: what being married to a drunkard is like; how *he* felt about his wife's distress. I also noticed how the poem's words became part of the 'history': 'her house is her cell', one audience member quoted back at me, making me consider my responsibility for the words I choose.

Anna's reflections reinforce the point that writing is not just the final step in historical research but an ongoing process of thinking, from the very start of a project, up until we communicate our work to audiences, and beyond. Each time we have presented work from our collaboration to different groups, people discover new things about the cases, as each person brings their own perspective to the material. We want to hold on to those many perspectives.

2.4 Use the Whole Page

We think about ways to adapt conventional forms of historical writing. Brenda Miller and Suzanne Paola coined the term 'hermit crab essay' to describe essays that 'appropriate existing forms as an outer covering'.[53] We have drawn on this idea to use a range of hermit crab forms: museum labels, maths equations, postcards, letters, questionnaires, or recipes. Rather than only the monovocal historical narrative, these different structures perform different functions. They do not simply state 'this is how things were'; they list, question, summarize, and translate.

Towards the end of the year working with Poppy and Anna, Will reflected on forms that could be borrowed for history writing:

In terms of poetry – and script writing – one thing that I hadn't thought enough about before was using the whole page. Both Anna and Poppy showed me how the page is not an empty space to be filled with text or meaning, which is often how historians treat it. We fill our pages up to the brim with words. If you open a history book, it normally looks like dense blocks of text, as much as possible squeezed into the space. Historians might ask themselves: why are things in certain places on the page? What are the different areas I could be using? I want to think more about the reader encountering the page, the white space.

Within poetry, arguments for using the whole page have been rising and falling for more than a hundred years. In 1897, Mallarmé published his inspirational visual poem 'A Throw of the Dice Will Never Abolish Chance', describing it as a 'score' in which the page's 'blanks' are a 'surrounding silence'.[54] In concrete

---

[53] Brenda Miller and Suzanne Paola, *Tell It Slant: Creating, Refining and Publishing Creative Nonfiction* (New York: McGraw-Hill, 2019), 312–14.

[54] Stéphane Mallarmé, 'Un coup de dés jamais n'abolira le hasard'. https://bit.ly/3Jag391.

and visual poetry, there is no clear linear progress through the poem; the reader has to consciously navigate the page, making active choices about where the eye falls. More recently, environmentally engaged poets like Harriet Tarlo advocate using the 'landscape' of the whole page, privileging sound, spatial arrangement, and uncertainty in 'open-field poetics'.[55]

The conventions of academic historiographical page layout, by contrast, are straightforward. In general, the main body of the page presents narrative or analysis organized into paragraphs of roughly equal size, covering as much of the page as possible. Footnotes or endnotes provide references to substantiate the claims made in the text, allowing the reader to follow up the research process and readings that the author has undertaken. Sometimes these notes also include asides, where the author speaks more directly to the reader.

Histories do not have to be written in this format to be faithful to research. Drawing on poets' uses of the whole page, Will experimented with an 'open-field' piece of history. He explains:

> In the following piece, I have tried to position the words on the page relative to their factual certainty, from most certain on the left, to most speculative on the right. The historical material is framed by a piece on non-fiction methods and factual accuracy by the writer Roy Clark. Using the whole page allows me to speculate, while giving the reader a sense of what is most speculative, and what is best-grounded in evidence. It allows the piece to respect the uncertainty of the story:

Roy Clark says there are two rules of non-fiction.

Do not add. Do not deceive.[56]
Never put something into your story that hasn't checked out.[57]

        I struggle with this
        in crimes
        of extravagant fear
        Like the attack on Jacques M,
        by his neighbour Joseph A,
        who thought him a witch

                                                    I think.

---

[55] David Kennedy and Christine Kennedy, *Women's Experimental Poetry in Britain, 1970-2010: Body, Time and Locale* (Liverpool: Liverpool University Press, 2013), 115–25.

[56] Roy Peter Clark, 'The Line between Fact and Fiction', in Mark Kramer and Wendy Call (eds.), *Telling True Stories: A Nonfiction Writers' Guide from the Nieman Foundation at Harvard University* (New York: Plume, 2007), 164–9, 166,

[57] Clark, 'The Line between Fact and Fiction', 167.

Let's begin with just the facts then,
as spelled out by an

indictment
drawn up on 11 September 1886   [58]
by the Advocate General of the Assize Court of Dijon.

> (Like faithful
> non-fiction authors
> we will not change the order of this story.)

Jacques: works at the pottery factory in Pouilloux, 29.

Joseph: a wheelwright at the same pottery factory, 66, married.

The men were neighbours.

The scene unfolds on 28 April 1886.

> But even Roy Clark says
> there are 'many interesting exceptions,
> > grey areas
> > that ... test' the
> > line between

non-fiction   [59]
                                        and fiction.

> Facts that are,
> in themselves,
>   fuzzy.

The indictment says
the scene unfolds on 28 April,
>   around midday, *perhaps.*

>   and how can
>   this
>   be a fact?
>   So vague.

The indictment continues
> After lunch
> (to use another fuzzy probability).

>   Now
>   if this detail is important,
>   its importance is not quite factual.

Does it matter
exactly when
it happened?

---

[58] Archives départementales de la Saône-et-Loire, 2 U 738.

[59] Clark, 'The Line between Fact and Fiction', 169.

Perhaps

not.

But

it surely matters

that it was after

lunch.

Did they

drink wine with lunch? Did Joseph have

an

argument with his wife? Did she tell

him she was

sick of this filth,

that

it was time to do

something

about it?

I am adrift

in speculation, but

perhaps

that has always been necessary

to historians.

Where an anthropologist

a journalist

can go back to eyewitnesses

with

new questions,

most historians cannot.

They operate,

by necessity,

in the field of 'historical possibilities',

even 'embellishments'

or 'creative assumptions'.[60]

But what everyone
can agree is that on

28 April 1886
Jacques met Joseph
on the road
between his house and the factory.

---

[60] 'Historical possibilities' is the phrase used by Natalie Zemon Davis and quoted in Carlo Ginzburg, 'Proofs and Possibilities: Postscript to Natalie Zemon Davis, *The Return of Martin Guerre*', reprinted in *Threads and Traces*, 54–71, 55. 'Embellishments' and 'creative assumptions' are two of the phrases Kiera Lindsey uses in the afterword to her 'biography' *The Convict's Daughter: The Scandal That Shocked a Colony* (Crow's Nest, NSW: Allen and Unwin, 2016), 284–5.

Probably
about 100 m from Jacques' house.
            Give or take.
It seems they were on their way back to work.
(This must be considered merely probable,
because only one of the men will ever make it to work that day)

            And yet again
            the importance of this likely detail
            is hardly in the fact itself.
            What
            a striking time to commit a crime:
            so ordinary and so routine,
            as if
            the criminal
            has timed his
            moment,
            plotted his crime.
Indeed,
this is what the prosecutor will want to suggest.

                                    But I'm the one who can't
                                    be trusted?

            So.

            What if
            the inclusion of this 'fact'
            is less about accuracy
            than about
            narrative?
            What if the story actually has precedence over the true
            details that will be
            observable
            recordable?

and then Joseph
fired
a
gun
at
Jacques
wounding
him
in
two
places.

        so
two shots were fired.
            Dare I

make some interpretation
of the attacker's state of mind,
an interpretation
that cannot possibly
ever
be factual,

> not just because he will
> – most likely –
> lie,
> or at least forget. No,
> there is no way to know his mind even if
> – in a moment of contrition –
> Joseph decides
> to come
> clean.

>> Which means
>> perhaps
>> the most important aspect
>> of this scene,
>> the most basic thing that
>> any novelist
>> would be able, obliged even,
>> to write,
>> the murderer's state of mind
>>
>> eludes the historian.
>>> (me)

> Perhaps he fired twice
> because
> his hand was unsteady.
> Perhaps he did not really want
> to kill his victim.
> A confrontation, not an
> execution. Perhaps it was meant
> to be a warning, not a punishment.

>> There is little from the
>> indictment to suggest this.
>> It does not, in Clark's terms,
>> 'check out'.

The consequences of using the whole page are broader than Will's intentions. It not only works to signal fidelity, plausibility, and speculation to the reader, but also patterns the unfolding of the narrative. Where the 'factual' details cluster, as in the moment of the shooting itself, the text is forced to huddle on the factual side of the page, as if the key moment is unfolding in slow motion. The distance on the page between the certain details and the historian's speculation becomes space for the reader to think, and to disagree.

Yet in many ways, Will's piece conforms to academic historical writing conventions. It uses quotation marks and footnotes to refer the reader to primary sources and secondary readings. This is not the only way to combine the body text with accompanying notes.

2.5 Play with Footnotes

In *The Body Multiple*, the anthropologist Annemarie Mol works to situate her ethnographic study of one hospital in 'the literature' by other researchers. Rather than hiding this relationship 'between the lines' of her whole text, she took the decision to divide the book into two: the ethnography runs across the top half of the page, and the 'literature' appears below, 'in a series of separate texts that resonate, run along, interfere with, alienate from, and give an extra dimension to the main text. In a subtext, so to speak'.[61]

Anna reads historical texts like a poet. She explains:

> When I was reading a particularly dense article, I found my eyes straying to the footnotes.[62]

Historians sometimes see footnotes as scaffolding – in Anthony Grafton's explanation, 'part of an effort to counter skepticism about the possibility of attaining knowledge about the past'.[63] They do not work like this in poems. Will reflects:

> When Anna adds a historical footnote to one of her draft poems, I feel that it tampers with the mystery of the poem-world. A poem is good at gesturing, at leaving things unsaid. I worry that the footnote explains too much, it bursts the poem's bubble.

Anna feels differently about what the notes do. She says:

> Sometimes, I don't just want to feel in a poem, I want to think.
> I find myself hooked in by poetry collections that foreground their historical sources. The footnote / side note / source-note becomes part of the visual world of the poem on the page. In *Ormonde*, Hannah Lowe tells the story of a

---

[61] Annemarie Mol, *The Body Multiple: Ontology in Medical Practice* (Durham, NC: Duke University Press, 2002), 3.

[62] They are bite-sized.
They are distracting.
Something about their small font is appealing. They give my eyes a little rest from the main body of text and my mind a little rest from its argument.
The footnotes remind me of one of my children, pulling on my sleeve and whispering in my ear, while I'm trying to conduct a serious conversation with an adult.

[63] Anthony Grafton, *The Footnote: A Curious History* (Cambridge: Harvard University Press, 1997), 24.

ship that is a footnote in history – the forgotten 'first ship' that arrived in the UK from Jamaica before the *Empire Windrush*. Her historical notes sit on the page with the poem; your eye travels back and forth between news clippings, poetry, and historical information.[64]

In *Famished*, Cherry Smyth collages 'lyrical poetry with statistics, quotes, newspaper cuttings, snippets of conversation and even nursery rhymes' to tell the story of the Irish Famine.[65] Ocean Vuong's 'Seventh Circle of Earth' is a blank-page poem comprised only of footnotes, written in response to a horrific homophobic crime. Vuong's subversive act is to inhabit the footnotes.[66]

Poppy adds:

These poems show me that footnotes are not just about adding content or part of a process of knowledge accumulation. The footnote can draw attention to the gap – to what is felt to be missing.

Anna responds:

It was this 'noticing the gap' that inspired my own experiments with footnoting. I wondered what might be missing in witchcraft cases that we might want to notice … I worked with a newspaper report about a shooting that took place in 1906 in Paris.

2.6 Case Study 2: Paris, 1906

The twenty-seven-year-old Juliette Granèche, *Le Journal* explained, had become a close friend of Marie Lhériteau, fifteen years her senior. Lhériteau initiated Granèche into magical practices including contacting the spirits of the dead, as well as using candles to curse and even kill an enemy. So, when Granèche's luck turned sour, she blamed her misfortune on Lhériteau. The younger woman went to the older woman's apartment and shot her five times with a revolver.

Anna turned this report into a footnote poem. The main body of the text quotes directly from the news story, and the notes at the bottom of the page talk back:

---

[64] Hannah Lowe, *Ormonde* (London: Hercules Editions, 2014).

[65] Cherry Smyth, *Famished* (Glasgow: Pindrop Press, 2019).

[66] Vuong writes: 'I hope that the form speaks, enacts, also, that for those in the margins who are perennially silenced, the footnote can be a place one gets to tell one's story. That because the main stage has been obliterated does not mean all hope of speech is lost. And perhaps taking over the primary space is not the only method, and that changing or charging the forgotten space, the after-thought, with new power is also a subversive possibility.' Ocean Vuong, 'How I Did It: Forward First Collection Special – Ocean Vuong on "Seventh Circle of Earth"'. https://bit.ly/3D0MZ1j.

Text from the newspaper article 'A Spiritualist Tragedy', *Le Journal*, 19th April 1906

close friendship[1] sprang up

enchantment using wax figurines[2]

four shots to the chest[3]

discharged revolver[4] in her hand

bathed in her own blood[5]

by means of the candle flame[6]

---

[1]   I wish my eyes were hazel just like yours
       for I am a nesting doll
       with many doll-souls
       inside me growing smaller and smaller

       While my staring eyes admit
       your magic lies
       my doll-souls blink
       and sharpen their resolve

[2]   Does your dolly have my face, my flaws?
       Does your dolly know what I may endure?
       The evening is enchanted.
       I shall cross the Bois de —

[3]   Your heart is
       held in a bodice
       boned like a pigeon-breast
       1234 take your own sweet time
       over your last out-breath
       the bellows, the pump, the ribs
       the ribbons all prettily undone

       you may huff and puff and
       blow my candle-flame out
       I will use my

[4]   gun

[5]   shot-silk
       enough to fill a tub
       I always thought red
       a funny choice of colour
       for a day-dress

[6]   little dolly melts
       a candle puddled down

Figure 1 Anna's poem 'A Spiritualist Tragedy'

There is a playfulness in how the poem uses footnotes. The notes actually take up more of the page than the main body of the text. They tell their own stories, or interject with correctives or clarifications. Anna uses this as a way to incorporate the variety of sources she has drawn on into the pages of the poem:

> Playing with footnotes, I might demonstrate visually how my work collaborates with its historical sources; undermining the explanatory narrative, untelling the story, adding feeling and *other* points of view.

Poetry, a form that is mostly met by its reader on the page, can make use of footnotes like any other type of writing. It can be more challenging for playwrights to convey this in live performance, and not just in their printed scripts. In Alecky Blythe's work, which she terms 'recorded delivery', the actors wear earpieces on stage through which they hear the original interviews which the piece is based on, in order to mimic them as accurately as possible. These earpieces are like visible footnotes for the audience, only they cannot hear what the notes include. In some of her plays, Blythe herself speaks to the audience as a narrator, explaining how the play has been put together.[67] Poppy points out that, in a similar way:

> Perhaps the footnote could appear as an extra character – a historian who constantly interrupts the characters on stage, or arrives at the end of scenes to dispute, challenge, or clarify what has already been said.

In the following extract by Will uses the device of a play within a play. The characters on stage play the researcher-writers (us) playing the historical actors:

WILL: So, I'm the judge, Poppy is Molleton, Anna is me? Ok? (*Pause*). Ahem. (*Solemn*). Mademoiselle Molleton –

ANNA: Actually, it's Malleton.

WILL: Hang on, are you playing **me** interrupting the actual judge, who really was actually there, to tell him he got the name wrong in court?

ANNA: Well, yes. You told me. I mean **you**, Will, the historian, you told **me** Anna the poet when I was researching this case that the name was different in the judgement you found in the archives in Lyon.

WILL: Yes, but the judge **said** Molleton.

---

[67] Alecky Blythe, 'Alecky Blythe', in Will Hammond and Dan Steward (eds.), *Verbatim, Verbatim: Contemporary Documentary Theatre* (London: Oberon, 2012), 77–102.

POPPY: Well the **newspaper account said he said** Molleton. Didn't you
            tell us before that sometimes they got things wrong?

WILL: So we're going to change the only written source we have for what
            happened in court?

ANNA: Well. Yes. But we're changing it to be **more** accurate.

The play within a play device can serve, as Freddie Rokem has argued, as 'an epistemological critique' and as 'a measure for the dialectic between the real and the fantastic'.[68] A scene like this may not literally be able to incorporate footnotes, but its reflexivity allows the script to perform some of the same functions. It points to sources and origins, and signals the work that the creative representation does to remain faithful to historical events, while staging its own fallibility.

Like the other techniques this section has explored, this dramatic reflexivity does not simply tell the audience what 'really happened'. It uses creative methods to make visible the problems of deciding which version of events to believe. In this way, techniques such as borrowed forms, using the whole page, and playing with footnotes all build on the fundamental idea of writing to discover. They do not provide audiences with fixed accounts of what the magic in these cases might be, instead inviting us as readers, and as writers, to constantly question what actually happened.

2.7 Exercises

Take some notes after you do each exercise. What does it bring to your thinking? What did you find challenging and why? Treat the exercises as fun, and as thinking.

1. Find materials.
    a. This works best with at least one other person, and even better a group of people.
    b. Choose a short textual primary source (one page). If you are looking for inspiration from the histories of magic, you could try looking at online databases, such as Early English Books Online, which includes pamphlets about English witch trials.
    c. Share your source with the group. What drew you to it? What do others make of it?
    d. You can use this 'found' material for many of the exercises in this Element. Try concentrating on one source for many exercises.

---

[68] Freddie Rokem, *Performing History: Theatrical Representations of the Past in Contemporary Theatre* (Iowa City: University of Iowa Press, 2000), 38.

2. Experiment with footnotes. Where might you include notes on the original text? You could use your own example source, or one that someone else has shown you.

    a. Spend ten minutes adding notes that explain or gloss the text. If you are working in a group, you can discuss what you have been doing.

    b. Spend ten minutes adding notes that contradict, question, or undermine the text.

    c. Read back over the notes you have added. If you are working in a group, you can discuss the following questions: Do the notes themselves tell a story? Do you want to explore that story in more detail?

    d. Write for ten minutes about what you learned from the exercise. Did you change your mind about aspects of the source? Do you have new questions?

3. Write about your source using a 'hermit crab form'.

    a. Try writing about it as a list. How should it be organized? What would you list from the source?

    b. Reframe your source as a letter. Who are you writing to and why?

    c. If you are working with a group, experiment with translating each other's pieces into other forms: make a list a script; make a letter a recipe; make a script a poem.

4. Write about your source using the whole page.

    a. You could start with one of the hermit crab forms you have already written. Or you could start a new piece. Spend ten minutes experimenting with moving the text to different parts of the page. Develop your own rules.

        i. Perhaps the top of the page is for things that are obvious, and the bottom is for things that are submerged or hidden.

        ii. Or perhaps you want to try organizing the page from left to right from agreed facts, through possibilities, to speculation.

        iii. Or blow your text apart. Imagine the page as a landscape. Put more blank space into what you have written, add line breaks, and fragment phrases and sentences across the page.

3 Brevity

...historians, determined by their documentation, grasp sorcery only as a white space in the *margins* of writing and its text.[69]

---

[69] Michel de Certeau, *The Writing of History*, trans. Tom Conley (New York: Columbia University Press, 1988), 290.

Your job is to undo the adhesiveness of the evidence you've gathered,
Its tendency to clump into indissoluble units.
Dissolve them.[70]

3.1 The Problem

Witchcraft is constituted of fragments and silences.[71]

Witches themselves were thought to work in secret. This is both one of the reasons that witchcraft was thought so dangerous and also the reason why 'witches' so rarely speak in sources from the nineteenth and twentieth centuries. Jeanne Favret-Saada doubts they really existed. Witches, she points out, 'never recognize themselves as such', and 'have no position from which to speak'.[72] Being bewitched, on the other hand, was clearly an experience that people could sometimes admit to. But even the bewitched were enjoined to silence. They dared not speak to the authorities and knew they must not speak to the witch.[73] To admit to involvement in secretive magical practices remained dangerous even after 'witchcraft' was definitively decriminalized.[74] Also, the very sources in which the historian finds witchcraft cases actively work to censor and suppress mention of what they often saw as dangerous primitive survivals. In the age of the newspaper, the authorities worried that court cases might bring attention to these regrettable beliefs, and publicity to magic practitioners. Some criminal cases were heard in closed sessions, with no public audience. In other cases, the official judicial records leave the word 'witchcraft' out as completely as they can, only mentioning the criminal offence of 'fraud' or 'illegal medical practice'. In one case from 1837 in Blainville-Credon, the judgement against a man accused of fraud is filled with ellipses, referring to 'several little books that the man claimed contained his … ' and magical 'practices' that are referred to as 'namely … '.[75] These 'named' practices are paradoxically *un*named.

The problem of historical silences is particularly visible and powerful in the case of modern witchcraft, but it is also a problem of much broader reach. Gaps and omissions are, as Michel-Rolph Trouillot puts it, 'inherent in history'.

---

[70] Klinkenborg, *Several Short Sentences*, 123.

[71] William G. Pooley, 'Can the "Peasant" Speak? Witchcraft and Silence in Guillaume Cazaux's "The Mass of Saint-Sécaire', *Western Folklore* 71:2 (2012), 93–118.

[72] Favret-Saada, *Deadly Words*, 125.

[73] Bouteiller, *Sorciers et jeteurs de sorts*, 96; Jeanne Favret-Saada, 'Unbewitching as Therapy', *American Ethnologist* 16:1 (1989), 40–56, 46. For one example among many from the project, see Pierre D's testimony in a case from 1844 heard in Valence, where an unwitcher instructed him and his wife to perform a series of actions in complete silence and secrecy: *Gazette des Tribunaux*, 19 April 1844.

[74] On the eighteenth-century precedents for secrecy, magic, and danger, see Krampl, *Les secrets des faux sorciers*, 63–4, 125–7.

[75] See Archives Départementales de la Seine-Maritime, 3 U 4 1323.

'Something is always left out while something else is recorded.'[76] Historians have often presented their work as an attempt to fill these silences: they 'read against the grain' to give voice to the silenced historical majority.[77] Building on the work that archivists have already done to collate and collect sources, historians research *around* these scraps to provide context, but also to unify different examples, to summarize and collate them, to discover a macrocosm from some microcosms. From the counting impulses of social history to the more recent distant-reading techniques of digital humanities, there is a compulsion to treat fragments as parts of a puzzle to be reconstituted. Even so-called 'microhistories' – which excavate the story of an individual, often unknown, or a minor or very brief event, or one object – work to salvage and repair these fragments and to turn scattered information about their microcosm into coherent stories.[78] 'Rich', 'detailed', and 'exhaustive' are positive adjectives to describe historical narratives, while 'thin' or 'patchy' histories are criticized for the gaps and omissions that they betray.

There are dangers in a model of historical writing that focuses on exhaustiveness. If magic operates through silence, why not use silence to write about magic? What can very short forms of history do that longer ones cannot? Historians might sometimes need to resist the urge to fill gaps, to interpret or speculate about what is missing. Instead, they can learn from creative writers how to 'erase' historical sources, make space for silence, write fragments, and accumulate short pieces of writing. We use these techniques on a case from 1890, where a young woman killed her newborn child, claiming she did so under the control of a 'witch'.

3.2 Case Study 3: Saint-Saëns, 1890

Stéphanie Adolphine Vatinel was a twenty-one-year-old house servant in the town of Saint-Saëns in Normandy. At the end of 1889, neighbours had begun to notice that the young woman appeared to be pregnant, but whenever the subject was raised, she insisted she was not.

On the 29th of March, she gave birth in the kitchen where she worked, and the baby fell into a bucket between her legs. At first, Vatinel claimed the baby was stillborn, but confronted with the body of the infant, she

---

[76] Trouillot, *Silencing the Past*, 49.

[77] For a nice example of this 'reading' of silence, see Julie-Marie Strange, 'Reading Language as a Historical Source', in Simon Gunn and Lucy Faire (eds.), *Research Methods for History* (Edinburgh: Edinburgh University Press, 2016), 193–209.

[78] The paradigmatic example is Carlo Ginzburg, *The Cheese and the Worms: The Cosmos of a Sixteenth-Century Miller* (Baltimore, MD: Johns Hopkins University Press, 1992). See also István M. Szijártó and Sigurður Gylfi Magnússon, *What is Microhistory? Theory and Practice* (London and New York: Routledge, 2013).

confessed that she had strangled it and hidden the body. A charge of infanticide was quickly drawn up against the young woman, but the trial was delayed after the investigating judge ordered three medical experts to produce a report on her mental state. Vatinel had not only behaved oddly in the run-up to the crime but had also raised difficult questions about the culpability of her co-worker, Pascal-Émile Bastide. According to Vatinel, not only was Bastide the father of the infant, but he had exerted a magical power over her which had allowed him to seduce her and also prevented her from realizing she was pregnant until the very last moment. He had told her that she was not pregnant but simply had a 'ball of water' in her stomach. She said that she had believed him and had also feared the magical books he kept in his pocket and his ability to predict the future.

As in the 1886 Pouilloux case discussed in the last section, the Saint-Saëns infanticide became a contest over narratives. Was Vatinel telling the truth about what she had believed? Could she really have been so naïve about her own pregnancy? Was she a 'hysteric' whose actions had been controlled through hypnotic suggestion by her alleged seducer, Bastide, as some medical authorities argued? This was what the court eventually decided. On the doctors' advice, Vatinel was acquitted, provoking discussion in newspapers across the whole country.

There is a neatness to this conclusion that is out of keeping with the confused testimonies of the witnesses, and especially of Vatinel herself. Laura Gowing has argued that witnesses and accused in similar early modern English infanticide cases 'told stories that obscure as much as they reveal'.[79] Where the court and newspapers sought narrative resolution, we are interested in the silencing and absences that run through the case. Rather than her 'story' – which never seemed to fully satisfy the doctors, or Vatinel herself – what was it that she was unable to say, or to admit to herself?

3.3 Erase the Sources

We apply an 'uncreative' technique that runs counter to all of the historian's instincts: we erase the sources.[80] Mary Ruefle has described 'erasure' poetry as:

> the creation of a new text by disappearing the old text that surrounds it … I
> call them erasures, but elsewhere they have been referred to as elision books,

---

[79] Laura Gowing, 'Secret Births and Infanticide in Seventeenth-century England', *Past & Present*, 156:1 (1997), 87–115, 89.

[80] See Kenneth Goldsmith, *Uncreative Writing: Managing Language in the Digital Age* (New York: Columbia University Press, 2011).

hyper-editing, cross-outs, and, my least favorite of all these unfavorites, 'creative defacement.' They are texts made by getting rid of, in a thousand and one ways, surrounding, pre-existing text.[81]

The poet Tracy K. Smith produced an erasure poem based on the American Declaration of Independence. By deliberately removing phrases that anchor the original document in the period of the American Revolution, Smith performs what she calls an act of 'time travel', linking the grievances of the founding fathers to other grievances that have been silenced in that history – those of enslaved people – and to the injustices of racism in contemporary America. Smith says that 'going to a document or a text that has lived in one context or one time and seeking to hear something new within it is, to me, seeking to hear what that document has to say about the present context and the present time'. She suggests this is 'history as an act of repair':

He has plundered our –

       ravaged our –

              destroyed the lives of our –

taking away our – [82]

Taking text away can paradoxically be a way to reveal meanings that are not obvious in the whole source. It reveals connections, subtexts, and meanings that were silenced in the original document.

In a similar way, M. NourbeSe Philip's book-length poem *Zong!* explores 'the many silences within the Silence' of a historical text, a legal decision about the deliberate massacre of 150 enslaved Africans in 1781 by the captain of the Zong, who believed this would allow the owners to claim an insurance payout. Philip sees herself as 'giving voice' in her poem not via imaginative addition but rather by noticing 'voices surfacing in the text': 'it is a work of haunting, a wake of sorts, where the spectres of the undead make themselves present'.[83]

Her poem emphasizes disjunctures, gaps, and confusion, and re-enacts the violence of the historical event itself:

> I murder the text, literally cut it into pieces, castrating verbs, suffocating adjectives, murdering nouns, throwing articles, prepositions, conjunctions overboard, jettisoning adverbs: I separate subject from verb, verb from object – create semantic mayhem, until my hands bloodied, from so much killing and cutting, reach into the stinking, eviscerated innards, and like some seer, sangoma, or prophet who, having sacrificed an animal for signs and

---

[81] Mary Ruefle, 'On Erasure', in *Quarter After Eight* 16 (n.d). www.ohio.edu/cas/quarter-after-eight/table-contents#on.

[82] Tracy K. Smith, 'Declaration'. 2018. https://bit.ly/3JAgIk3.

[83] M. NourbeSe Philip and Setaey Adamu Boateng, M. *Zong!* (Middletown, CT: Wesleyan University Press, 2011), 201.

Figure 2 Extract from Anna's poem 'JG'

portents of a new life, or simply life, reads the untold story that tells itself by not telling.[84]

There are many different ways to erase any given text. Mary Ruefle erases impressionistically, picking the words that stand out visually to her 'as if they were flowers'.[85] Anna experiments with some more rule-based forms of erasure, such as erasing all of the words from a 1906 news story about Juliette Granèche, except those that contain the initials 'JG'.[86]

Anna reflects:

> The article delights in describing women toying with the occult, mocks the criminal (intimating she is a prostitute 'well-known in society') and categorizes her as a neurotic. Where is Juliette? By erasing in a pattern, the news story is *untold* and told anew. The totalizing journalist's story easily comes apart.
>
> I try to capture how when we study history, its characters might become huge to us, centralised in our minds, but they are also minute, impossible to understand, lost in time.

Anna tries the same exercise with the original French newspaper story, and then translates the erasure into English:[87]

young	Juliette Granèche	grace
	figurines candle	
	extinguished	
day	Juliette Granèche	longtime
intelligence	days	
	floor	
Juliette Granèche	Juliette Granèche unloaded	
lay	bathed	
	blood	
serious	Juliette Granèche	interrogated
judge	young	
thrown		

---

[84] NourbeSe Philip and Boateng, *Zong!*, 191, 193–4.   [85] Ruefle, 'On Erasure'.
[86] This is the 1906 case mentioned in the previous section.
[87] Which is why some words that have no 'J' or 'G' in English – such as candle – but do in French (*bougie*) appear in the poem.

Anna writes:

> My erasure centres Juliette, but foregrounds the limitations of words to tell her story. It doesn't presume to imagine and fill in her 'voice' and she remains silent. The white space of what we don't know, what we can't know, is more prominent than the words of the poem.

Will adopts a different methodical erasure to the 1890 Saint-Saëns case, inspired by Sarah Knott's 'verb-led' history of mothering. He removes everything except the verbs from a newspaper report in *Le Radical* 5th August 1890:

The newspaper announced Adolphine was charged.
Adolphine claimed to have obeyed.
Adolphine depicted, the court interrogated.
     The court postpones.
     The court allows the doctors conducting to conclude: Adolphine's responsibility was.

Adolphine appeared. Adolphine maintained. Adolphine had done.
     Adolphine strangled. Adolphine was.
     Adolphine gave birth.

Bastide told her it was a ball of water going away.
     A ball of water squeezed. Adolphine thought she was squeezing.
Bastide has denied, Bastide has said.
     Bastide claimed Bastide was.
     Bastide seems. Bastide reads. Bastide is not.
Bastide cannot read.
     Bastide courts, Bastide has relations.
     Did Bastide tell?

Adolphine claims Bastide did.
     Did Bastide make her drink?
     Bastide made her drink.
     Adolphine did not want to: the milk has not been strained.
Bastide forced Adolphine to drink.

Adolphine's employer gave evidence.
     Adolphine was, her employer said.
     Adolphine had, Adolphine laughed, Adolphine ran.
     Adolphine said Adolphine was told to be quiet or to leave.
Adolphine was quiet or left.
     Was Bastide?
Bastide did chase, Adolphine's employer noticed.

Adolphine and Bastide had taken a fancy to each other.

Had Adolphine?

Had Adolphine?

Adolphine was acquitted.

One effect of highlighting the verbs is to foreground the struggle over agency and responsibility in the case. Rather than actions, the poem emphasizes that the case is about narrations – the most common verbs are all about speaking and claiming, and even when the verbs involve other actions, they are often phrased as questions: had Adolphine? Another consequence is to defamiliarize the story. Adolphine becomes not just a tragic child-murderer, but a young woman who laughs and who runs. These verbs must be freed from their context to take on this meaning, because their context is the construction of Adolphine as a 'hysteric'. What if, instead, she had been happy? What if all of her experiences were not defined by the murder of her child? At the same time, a different context emerges from these untethered verbs: Adolphine's obedience. The verbs emphasize who was 'told', how she 'obeyed'. Even stripped back to the verbs, Adolphine resists talking of her own actions as her own choices.

This paradox of subtraction is similar to the paradoxical effects of short form writing: the more we leave out, the more weight each word seems to carry.

3.4 Case Study 4: Place Hébert, 1906

We experiment with what very short written forms can do with another case, which appeared in *Le Matin*, 16th May 1906.

A crowd of indignant mothers and impassioned children had formed yesterday afternoon, on the place Hébert, at la Chapelle, around a girl in tears who was screaming pitifully. A policeman passing by thought it his duty to elucidate the cause of this disturbance.

He questioned the little girl, who finally confessed that her mother was in the habit of beating her for no reason and that she had just engaged in this exercise.

Several women present confirmed this story, ensuring that they had seen her beat the child who had escaped from the hands of her torturer.

Armed with this information, the policeman looked for this unnatural mother. He eventually found her, sitting calmly on a bench, away, in a corner of the square, seemingly nothing to do with the scandal she had in fact caused. She was driven to the police station, through the jeering of the sensitive souls of the neighbourhood.

M. Pontaillier, police commissioner, questioned her.

And the answers surprised him. Because Ernestine Lejeune (the name of this housewife living in Plaine-Saint-Denis) asserted, in her defence, that the overwhelming blows she constantly dealt out to her daughter were the only means of countering the fatal influence of a spell once cast upon the girl by an evil witch.

She talked at length on this subject with such an abundance of incoherent remarks that the magistrate was easily convinced that he was dealing with a madwoman. As a result, Ernestine Lejeune was sent to the special infirmary.

As for the unfortunate girl, she was sent to the orphanage.[88]

3.5 Write Short

When dealing with this source, which in many ways is opaque to us, we make a virtue of brevity. Anna writes:

> Reading the newspaper account, I was struck by its description of the ostra-cized mother sitting alone on a bench in a city square, while a group of local women called the police. In this fragment of text, with no 'backstory' for Ernestine's situation, it is difficult to empathize or make sense of her violent actions, and our immediate sympathy is for the abused child.
>
> It struck me that the isolated and ostracized female in this story is not a witch, but a woman who fears witchcraft. I wanted to join her, imaginatively, on that bench. To do so, I connected to my experiences of the emotional difficulties and isolation that can be attendant on being a mother. This is a hard-to-approach feeling and topic, and as such, is suited to the very brief form I chose for this piece entitled 'Among the Many Mothers':

I am lonely
as
that mother
sitting alone

on a bench
in Place Hébert

the one who tried
to beat the curse
out of her
daughter

and so
lost her

Many mothers
do bad things

me
too

---

[88] *Le Matin*, 16 May 1906.

Compared to the original news story above, the gaps on the page remind the reader that if Ernestine 'talked at length', none of her own words are actually reproduced by the journalist. But rather than reading into the gaps in the newspaper story, Anna's poem adopts the same terse style. The sparse text emphasizes the emotional weight, or even culpability, that the words imply.

This is the paradox of brevity described above: the more we leave out, the more weight each word seems to carry. Concise forms force intimacy with the past. They put the reader in the midst of things: 'The poem', Mary Oliver has written, 'is not a discussion, not a lecture, but an *instance* – an instance of attention, of noticing something in the world'. Oliver gives the example of William Carlos Williams' 'The Red Wheelbarrow', an eight-line poem of just sixteen words total:

> What does its apparent simplicity mean? Perhaps that for [William Carlos Williams] a poem is not a matter of some serious predetermined subject, but of concentrated focus and attention upon an 'ordinary' simple subject – a mere scene – then, through the elevation of art, the scene is lifted into the realm of something quite extraordinary and memorable.[89]

Short writing focuses attention onto every individual word. This weightiness has multiple consequences. What Lia Purpura calls 'miniatures' are 'the familiar, reduced to unfamiliarity. Miniatures are improbable, unlikely. Causes to marvel. Surprises. Feats of engineering. Products of an obsessive detailer'.[90] Words that bear all of this weight can also project a solidness and power. 'Poems can be', in Jesse Nathan's words, 'moments of stillness'.[91]

Consider haiku. These poems normally consist of three lines, with five syllables in the first line, seven in the second line, and five in the final line.

> Often focusing on images from nature, haiku emphasizes simplicity, intensity, and directness of expression. [They often include a] focus on a brief moment in time; a use of provocative, colorful images; an ability to be read in one breath; and a sense of sudden enlightenment.[92]

In an article from the early twentieth century encouraging American poets to try this Japanese form, the poet Yone Noguchi compared the haiku to:

> a tiny star … carrying the whole sky at its back. It is like a slightly-open door, where you may steal into the realm of poesy. It is simply a guiding lamp. Its value depends on how much it suggests.[93]

---

[89] Mary Oliver, *A Poetry Handbook* (San Diego, CA: Harcourt Brace and Company, 1994), 72–4, 74.

[90] Lia Purpura, 'On Miniatures'. https://bit.ly/36kl94e.

[91] Dorothea Lasky, Dominic Luxford, and Jesse Nathan, *Open the Door: How to Excite Young People about Poetry* (San Francisco, CA: McSweeney's, 2013).

[92] Academy of American Poets, 'Haiku'. https://poets.org/glossary/haiku.

[93] Yone Noguchi, 'A Proposal to American Poets', *The Reader* 3:3 (1904), 248.

What can this practice do as historical writing? Anna was interested in the notes Will keeps as summaries of the cases he has researched. She uses haiku as a

> way of responding to the historian's notes in a way that preserves their form – their brevity. With the haiku I don't try to make meaning from the source – I don't embellish it or imagine it – I simply try to mirror it poetically. A haiku holds one story, one moment. It leaves a lot unanswered, as do the original historical notes:

> 1805
> She hurt our baby
> with her spell. Beggar lady
> strip her, torture, burn.[94]

It is a challenge to explain cases briefly when writing with the conventions of the historical third-person, as the following example by Will demonstrates:

> 1892
> Our crops ruined, stones,
> Explosions, the barn burnt down
> Our bloody son's fault![95]

Will reflects:

> I am forced into a closer point of view. I write in the voice of the people involved. To save words, the emotion is carried in the details, a barn burned, crops ruined. With the narrative simplicity of one turn, the haiku transforms the rather dull summaries, finding their essence, the key point of the story. They distil what is important, even from these very short texts.

Anna explained that the last line of a haiku poem is often used as a contrast, as a surprise, or in juxtaposition with the first two. Poppy was struck by this idea, writing that

> using just a few syllables, it becomes possible not only to capture the essential kernel of the historical cases, but also to invoke their contradictions, tensions and historical aporias too:

> 1891
> Can you hear a croak?
> There's a toad in your tummy.

---

[94] From Will's notes: 'Ménil (Ardennes). 2nd April 1805 (12 germinal an XIII) An old beggar-woman tortured, stripped, and burned for casting a spell on a baby'.

[95] La Solitude, near Le Mans (Sarthe). The Bigot family believe they are bewitched, with the witches not only ruining the crops but even throwing stones at them, setting off fireworks, and eventually burning down their barn. It turns out the culprit is their fourteen-year-old son. See *Le Petit Parisien*, 18 September 1892. The son was put in prison. See *Le Courrier du Centre* 20 September 1892.

Pay up. Toad leaps out.

These flashes, or instances, can be a way to get up close to the stories. Rather than the big picture of enduring myths about witchcraft and persecution, the haiku engage with momentary things that can be hard to capture. Anna suggests that:

> a strong narrative or clear causality is unsuited to the strangeness and unknowns of the witchcraft stories. Perhaps a series of glimpses such as those we provide in poetry and theatrical scenes is more effective. It leaves the unknowns unanswered.

They can also offer ways to jolt or to shock readers. Anna writes a haiku about a murder case:

> 1829
> Carafe of water
> reflects witch's face. Kill him.
> Your brother-in-law.

The haiku has the characteristic 'turn' between the second and third line: the identity of the witch comes as a shock, a twist on the story. Jolts like these work to give the past its future back. They make the outcome of the cases seem as unexpected as they must have been to many people at the time. Will tries another one:

> 1868
> 'I am bewitched', she says
> But the police decide her
> 'Possessed' of ... a child.

These jolts are one example of many from writing briefly that show how it focuses attention. Much like a theatre performance, they are constantly working to keep the audience's attention. As the playwright Stephen Jeffreys has put it:

> If you lose the audience, even for a minute, it's very hard to get them back, because they are holding on to a continuous piece of wire, they are following the story second by second. Our responsibility as playwrights is to make every single second interesting. This is our great problem, and also our great opportunity.[96]

3.6 Accumulate Fragments

The techniques of both erasure and short writing lend themselves to combinations. Instead of one long narrative or a coherent argument about the witchcraft

---

[96] Stephen Jeffreys, 'As a playwright, you must have something that you want to say', 2019. Nick Hern Books blog, https://bit.ly/34GeAIl.

cases, producing lots of small pieces is a way to stay with the specifics of each story, to linger on the unknown, and to present the big picture in little ways. The historian Sarah Knott has argued along similar lines in her 'anecdotal' history of mothering:

> Anecdote is a way of recasting … shards and nuggets of evidence, of turning absence into presence, what's mentioned *en passant* into the main drama.[97]

What value might there be in collages of anecdotes? Anna experiments with writing a whole series of haiku based on Will's summaries of the cases.

> 1792: So many devils / need to be exorcised, a / wave, call it a wave / 1796: Cattle sick again. / Unwitch them please. Cattle sick / again. Healing fraud. / 1803: I'm a surgeon trust / in me. I'll heal your girl – does / no training mean fraud? / 1803: Pact with the devil. / Hold onto his S-shaped horns. / Clouds smother the moon. / 1804: Fraud and *sorcier* / go hand in glove. At least in / the written records. / 1805: She hurt our baby / with her spell. Beggar lady / strip her, torture, burn. / 1805: Burn the old woman / who cannot, who will not, heal / this dying young man / 1806: Your tongue is on fire / when you call a housewife a / witch – cough up the fine / 1806: Murder for witchcraft. / No other details. Hate crime. / Nothing more to say. / 1807: Old man Pelet has / a bad reputation – witch. / Children murder him! / 1808: Veterinary witch- / craft. Spells may heal your livestock. / Your best things, made well. / 1809: Marc sets fire to / his master's farm. He believes / magic will dowse flames. / 1811: Swear I saw Louis / and friends dancing round devil's / table. Feast. Slander. / 1812: Is magic fraud if / it gets results? We only / hear from the failures. / 1813: Illegal practice / of medicine. Proceed to jail. / Many francs in fines. / 1815: A witch is murdered / by a sailor's family. / Unwitcher involved. / 1816: Man suspects wife of / cheating. Witch reveals name of / lover, who's shot dead. / 1818: Man poisoned by pear. / Decides vendor is a witch. / Cure: bite vendor's wife. / 1818: Entire village fears / a self-confessed witch, who owns / the book Dragon Rouge. / 1821: Man murdered by his / brothers during unwitching / ceremony. Why? / 1827: Face of thief who stole / a plate, revealed to servants. / Plate never returned. / 1828: He says he can heal / our babies. So weak, so ill. / Fraudulent magic. / 1829: Carafe of water / reflects witch's face. Kill him. / Your brother-in-law. / 1877: Witches are breaking / the crockery! Our cupboard / is cursed say grocers / 1884: Assault! Witch accused / of sending fleas to bite the / village's children. / 1887: Evil spirit haunts / house, makes cattle ill. Police / accuse prankster son. / 1892: If this rapist thinks / witchcraft and magic exist – / prison or madhouse?

The effect is almost deadening. Anna reflects:

> I think my haiku are quite creepy in their blankness. I think they refuse to engage too much with the possible emotions of the cases as they are too

---

focused on rendering the cases syllabically 5/7/5. And perhaps this actually tells us something about the difficulty of entering and comprehending these cases?

In Anna's collection of haiku, the same words come back to summarize different cases: fraud, fire, murder, crockery. The haiku convey something detailed about this repetitiveness of the cases that it can be very hard to communicate to audiences. For all the variation in details and individuals, many of the cases almost seem to follow the same scripts. Some of the individual haiku themselves express this sameness, this apparent inevitability: 'Cattle sick again. / Unwitch them please. Cattle sick / again.' Including the dates is another sad commentary on the continuities in the cases. But even in this depressing litany of misfortune and malice, Anna presents many cases as brief questions: 'prison or madhouse?' 'Does no training mean fraud?' 'Is magic fraud if it gets results?' 'Why?'

Where historians are very often tempted to get to the bottom of things, to solve mysteries, fill in gaps, and interpret silences, these techniques of erasure and short writing suggest ways to surprise ourselves with our materials. They provide jolts, instants of reflection, audible and visible silences. And in some ways they are closer to how witchcraft itself appears in historical sources. As Diane Purkiss has put it:

> The fragmentary narratives of witchcraft are already absurd; they are torn even where apparently most whole. [They are not an] articulate system [but a] set of half-formulated working rules.[98]

3.7 Exercises

Take notes about the experience of trying the exercises after you complete each one. Treat the exercises as a research process.

1. Erase a historical source. You could use one that you found using the exercise from the last section, or you could use the story of Ernestine Lejeune reproduced above.
   a. Erase the text instinctively, like Mary Ruefle, who describes her erasures of words as a visual experience, with the words floating off the page 'by say an eighth of an inch … singly and unconnected', like a field from which she picks 'words as if they were flowers'.[99]
   b. Or try grammatical erasures: erase the verbs, or the nouns, or leave only verbs or nouns.

---

[98] Purkiss, *The Witch in History*, 62.   [99] Ruefle, 'On Erasure'.

c. Try thematic erasures. Yedda Morrison's *Darkness*, for instance, is an erasure of Joseph Conrad's *Heart of Darkness*. Morrison leaves nothing but references to nature.[100]

2. Write a haiku: three lines – one of five syllables, the second of seven syllables, the third of five syllables. You could base your haiku on a found text, or use research notes or summaries. This exercise also works well with journal article abstracts.

   a. Try an online haiku generator (like this one: www.poem-generator.org .uk/haiku/) for inspiration.

   b. Write your own haikus. Try including a 'turn' or jolt between the second and third lines.

3. Write other short forms.

   a. You could try a 100-word theatrical monologue or poem. Give yourself five minutes. Try writing this about an instant when someone faces a life-altering moment (see https://fictionsoutheast.com/7-tips-for-writing-flash-fiction/).

      i. Once the writing is finished, take five more minutes to condense it to fifty words …

      ii. … then ten words …

      iii. … then five words.

   b. Write another piece about the same example. This time it can be as long as you like, but you have to write it in very short sentences.

      i. Verlyn Klinkenborg has some good tips for writing short sentences: avoid 'false syntax', words like 'with' and 'as', and 'floating, unattached phrases'. Instead, concentrate on strong verbs.

      ii. Re-read your piece and make the sentences even shorter. Klinkenborg is ruthless: 'remove every unnecessary word'.[101]

4. Accumulate fragments.

   a. Try a cento, a collage of lines collected from one or more source texts. What happens when you put these fragments next to one another? What new stories emerge?

   b. Try doing several haiku from the first exercise very quickly. Put a timer for ten minutes and see how many you can do.

---

[100] Yedda Morrison, *Darkness* (Los Angeles: Make Now Press, 2012).
[101] Klinkenborg, *Several Short Sentences*, 9–10, 12.

    i. It can also be rewarding to work intensively on one example for a longer period. How many different haiku examples can you create from one source text?

  c. Try arranging the short texts that you have produced for the exercises above into patterns on a page.

    i. Put them tightly packed together.

    ii. Space them out across the whole page.

4 Performance

The task for the historical writer is to take the past out of the archive and relocate it in a body.[102]

4.1 The Problem

We know that the sources we study to understand magic in the past are not the thing itself. One way to think about the gap between these textual remains and the past that they represent is performance: beyond words alone, how can we understand historical magic as a bodily or emotional practice? In the past, bodies have been experienced, moved, and constituted in other ways. Our ancestors felt feelings and emotions we no longer know.[103] Historical European witchcraft drew on bodily experiences and emotional connections that have often seemed alien and strange to modern writers: ideas about the 'fluxes' and fluids of the humoral body, where emotions, health, and spiritual influences were interchangeable.[104] This fluidity between categories continues into the modern French cases. To those who feared it, witchcraft quite literally is inappropriate emotion, malice, envy, or anger. But these emotions are contagious and dangerous, causing real bodily suffering, illness, or injury. For all its mystery, magic in these cases is resolutely concrete, touchable. Anthropologists in the twentieth century noted that witchcraft operated through breath, food, looks, and touches.[105]

---

[102] Hilary Mantel, 'Can These Bones Live?', *The Reith Lectures*, 2017. https://bit.ly/3wuAV77.

[103] See, for example, Knott, *Mother*, 88.

[104] This is a core theme of Roper, *Oedipus and the Devil* and Purkiss, *The Witch in History*, e.g. 119. See also Ulinka Rublack, 'Fluxes: the Early Modern Body and Emotions', *History Workshop Journal* 53:1 (2002), 1–16, and Barbara Duden, *The Woman Beneath the Skin: A Doctor's Patients in Eighteenth-century Germany*, trans. Thomas Dunlap (Cambridge, MA: Harvard University Press, 1991).

[105] All of these also appear in the project research. For a discussion of witchcraft as bodily actions, see also Bouteiller, *Sorciers et jeteurs de sorts*, 89–101.

Creative practices have a special role to play in researching past bodies and historical emotions. Theatrical performance, historical re-enactment, and even dressing up can be more-than-textual ways to know the past.[106] 'Theatre', Colette Conroy points out, 'is fundamentally concerned with the human body, and it also allows us to ask what we mean when we talk about bodies'. Performances disrupt the ordinariness of the body, the assumptions we constantly live with about our own bodies and the bodies of others. Bodies on stage are at once real and pretend: they always represent something – or someone – else.[107]

Improvisation can also help to defamiliarize, shaking us out of a misleading sense that we understand how people felt. Working like this may not provide definitive answers to research questions, but it expands our sense of what was possible and deepens our repertoires of empathy towards the people involved in witchcraft cases.

4.2 Re-enact

In 1831, a court in Premesques heard a slander case including accusations of witchcraft. At one point, a witness named Ignace Delmotte stood up to give evidence. Here is how a journalist reported Delmotte's testimony:

> Ignace Delmotte (this witness, who had bushy black sideburns trimmed like fortifications and the stature of a former Swiss Guard, appeared to avoid the plaintiff's gaze): 'I heard that Thérèse Delisle was a witch, that she could do tricks; I heard it from *Mimi* Coche who heard it from a woman who heard it from another woman who didn't hear it from anyone.' (*General prolonged laughter.*)

What is striking about the reporting is its theatricality. Like other court-reporters, the anonymous author of this piece provides detailed visual descriptions of witnesses, defendants, and victims. They try to reproduce the proceedings like a script, with attention to how words were spoken, what exactly was said, and how the audience responded. The 'accuracy' of this scene is hard to prove. Archived trial dossiers do not provide transcriptions of full court proceedings, for reasons that date back to the reforms of the justice system during the 1790s.[108] Also, the visual descriptions of participants in witchcraft cases often sound stereotyped or exaggerated. But these theatrical sources provoke us to ask: how can we recover all of the paratexts of stage directions, scene and setting, costume, and bodily movement?

---

[106] See Davidson, 'The Embodied Turn'.

[107] Colette Conroy, *Theatre and the Body* (Basingstoke: Palgrave Macmillan, 2010), 8, 20.

[108] Laura Mason, 'The "Bosom of Proof": Criminal Justice and the Renewal of Oral Culture during the French Revolution', *The Journal of Modern History* 76:1 (2004), 29–61.

One imaginative technique from theatre that historians can apply to sources that include dialogue is 'actioning'. Actioning a script involves identifying what each line of dialogue does. Rather than seeing the words people spoke in these cases simply as information, actioning invites historians to speculate about how words were said, and what they were meant to achieve.[109] In this way of seeing dialogue, words are always already actions. Marina Caladrone and Maggie Lloyd-Williams clarify that:

> An action, in this method, must be a transitive verb: 'a doing word' that you can actively do to someone else. It is always in the present tense and transitional, expressing an action that carries over from you (the subject) to the person you're speaking to (the object).[110]

This is a method that can throw up surprising results. What is explicitly said between characters does not necessarily correlate to the implicit emotions underlying a scene. Annotating a scene in this way involves a close reading, an attempt to think yourself into what the characters want. You cannot just read for the facts; you have to think yourself into the evolving intentions of the different characters.

In witchcraft, words are always actions. The most harmless greeting or a banal comment about the weather when meeting someone on the road could be interpreted as a veiled threat.[111] Certain 'actions' cluster around particular phrases: any compliment was liable to be interpreted as a threat and a statement of envy. What, then, can we learn from actioning a court scene from a newspaper report? We experiment with a case involving poltergeist phenomena from Lyon in 1861.

4.3 Case Study 5: Lyon, 1861

Two young women were accused of breaching the peace and disrespecting a police officer. The officer had been called out to the home of the Clavel family, who employed the two girls. For the last few months, the house had been under what Monsieur Clavel believed was a curse cast by a witch. Objects such as bobbins, bits of wood, and spit were thrown at the police, who eventually determined that the two girls were probably to blame. Will's annotations appear in square brackets on the newspaper's transcript of the interrogation of one of the girls below:

---

[109] Purkiss criticized historians for treating early modern witchcraft trials as repositories of information, rather than places where things happen. See *The Witch in History*, 71–2.

[110] Marina Caladrone and Maggie Lloyd-Williams *Actions: The Actors' Thesaurus* (London: Nick Hern Books, 2004), xvii.

[111] As in an attempted murder in Saint-Didier (Nièvre). See *Le Progrès de la Côte d'Or*, 24 April 1887.

Presiding judge. —	Mademoiselle Molleton, stand up. You have heard the witnesses, what do you have to say for yourself? [*to intimidate*]
The accused. —	I didn't throw anything, it was Mademoiselle Colon who couldn't help throwing things. [*to deflect*]
Presiding judge. —	And did you also throw them? [*to criticize*]
The accused. —	Just one bobbin. [*to mollify*]
Presiding judge. —	Indeed, you cannot deny it, because you were caught in the act. [*to support*]
The accused. —	I only ever threw that bobbin. [*to reassure*]
Presiding judge. —	Why did you want to make the Clavels believe this was the work of the devil? [*to cajole*]
The accused. —	No-one believed that, it was just a joke. [*to confuse*]

Will reflects:

> One of the things I wanted to do in 'actioning' this dialogue was to avoid repetition. Rather than the same intention for every utterance, I pushed myself to imagine both speakers having different purposes as they said each thing. Of course, this is artificial, but the result is that there is an evolution in the relationship between the judge and the young woman. At first, the judge intimidates and criticizes, but the deflection and mollification of Mademoiselle Molleton softens his attitude and they speak to reassure and support each another, as if they have come to an unspoken agreement to collaborate.
>
> I am not saying that the strangely tender relationship this suggests is the only – or even the most plausible – interpretation of the interrogation. But it encourages me to think differently about the case. For one, despite being on trial, Mademoiselle Molleton asserts her agency in this reading. It is she who deflects, mollifies, and reassures the judge, and her final action – to confuse – suggests she is the one controlling and directing the situation. This agency is denied by the words of the source itself: her defence is based, like Vatinel's in the 1890 Saint-Saëns case, on denying that she chose to act. This is a more subtle and complex understanding of the exchange than I think I could have come to simply by reading it.
>
> And beyond this, it forces me to reckon with the many different ways this scene could be actioned. I think that historians often ascribe motivation and intention to the words or actions of the people we study, only we do this silently, without spelling out our thinking, or indeed reflecting on the fact that what we are doing is interpreting their words in a particular way. Unquestioned, this silent 'actioning' naturalizes our assumptions.

Actioning dialogue from sources like this is a way to sketch out different possibilities. Crucially, it can work against the biases and assumptions we bring to our analysis of interactions in the past, inviting us to imagine other, more complex, possibilities in the sources we study. They are a form of structured improvisation.

4.4 Improvise

How far should we take such techniques of improvisation? Actioning is a method that remains close to the sources. What value might there be in more extreme improvisation?

We experiment with physical theatre, acting out the situations described in some of the cases. What things might the body, in Jacques Lecoq's words, know 'about which the mind is ignorant'?[112] Theatre and dance scholars argue for taking embodied practice seriously as a 'way of knowing', 'a system of learning, storing, and transmitting knowledge'.[113] We apply this to a simple example: many of the cases of violence involving witchcraft beliefs have as their starting point the chance meeting of two individuals on the road. Witnesses and participants focus on the intensity of this situation, and particularly on the power of eye contact. Poppy acted as director and asked Will and Anna to do some exercises working with eye contact. She told them to stand facing one another. Neither person could break eye contact. If they felt safe and comfortable, they should take a step towards the other person. If they felt at all uneasy, they should take a step back. Will reflected afterwards:

> It's difficult to overstate how hard this exercise was.
>
> It made me feel incredibly uncomfortable to stare into Anna's eyes for such a long period of time. How often would you do that? Only in very intense situations – I'm thinking of the relationship between an infant and a parent, or the way you might look into the eyes of a lover, or try to stare someone down in a violent confrontation. It feels very difficult to sustain, and the impulse to break eye contact is very strong.

Poppy told Anna and Will to try introducing some more movement to the scene. Like the historical individuals in the cases, this turned the eye contact into a meeting. How many different ways are there to meet someone on a road? Will was struck by just how different the interaction became with slight variations:

> We walked fast or slow, stopping in synchronicity, we tried to express different emotions with our bodies.
>
> It very quickly became a way to imagine the multiplicity of the witch encounters on the open road, the power of a look, the very real physicality of those situations.

---

[112] Jacques Lecoq, *The Moving Body: Teaching Creative Theatre*, trans. David Bradby (London: Methuen Drama, 2002), 9.

[113] Diana Taylor, *The Archive and the Repertoire: Performing Cultural Memory in the Americas* (Durham, NC: Duke University Press, 2003), 3, 16.

The exercise changed Anna's interest in Claudine, the wife of the murderer in the 1886 Pouilloux case, discussed above. Anna reflects:

> It fed into my imagining of Claudine having to visit the well and face hostile looks ... Then, in the days when I was reading about wells inMartine Segalen's book,[114] I collected my daughter from a playdate and the other mum showed me how their building work had uncovered the 'town well', still with water in it, underneath their kitchen. There was a strange serendipity, a time-travel, in finding myself physically standing on the edge of a well with another village woman, that put me in Claudine's shoes. When I told her about Claudine and the unnerving eye contact, she said, 'not so different from the school run then'.

Describing these insights textually might be beside the point. It is true that we can discuss examples of how bodily improvisation activities changed how we wrote and thought about the historical scenes we studied. They force us to think about them in space and in time. But by their very nature, many of these insights cannot be simply described in words: they are a change of perspective. They are the 'something other' that Rebecca Schneider refers to in her discussion of what re-enactment teaches re-enactors.[115]

Along with this bodily improvisation, we work on the role of props in performance, using examples from a case that took place in Vichy in 1935.

4.5 Case Study 6: Vichy, 1935

The case was reported by *Le Journal* as a possible hoax. The victims were a married and retired couple – the Griffets – who lived with their daughter and son-in-law. The first sign that something was not right in their household was the death of a calf, but this was soon followed by the mysterious demise of most of the family's chickens. In their distress, they called upon the services of a priest, who helped them to find a package that had been hidden in their chicken coop, containing 'crude' drawings, seeds, and needles. But the discovery of the package was only the start of their problems. In the days and weeks that followed, needles began to mysteriously appear in the house, in their food and drink, or hidden in clothing or pictures on the wall. Called back to the house, the priest sprinkled some holy water and scattered fragments of an Easter candle, which seemed to restore the calm:

---

[114] Segalen, *Love and Power.*

[115] Rebecca Schneider, *Performing Remains: Art and War in Times of Theatrical Reenactment* (London: Routledge, 2011), 14.

But the mystery endures.

Local know-it-alls say that the good folk of the Boutiron bridge have been victims of pranksters and the police seem to agree, as they are looking for the culprits. But the Griffet family have a cast-iron conviction that they were the victims of a witch.[116]

4.6 Use Dialogue

To translate the case into performance, Poppy's first step was to take the narrative bones of the newspaper story and transform them into dialogue. In the following scene, Poppy uses different characters to present different perspectives on what is happening:

Man. Woman. Son. Policeman.

1.

MAN:	Do you see them now?
WOMAN:	No.
SON:	Do you?
MAN:	No.
WOMAN:	What about you?
SON:	No.
WOMAN:	Can we just have another search for them?
SON:	We've spent all night searching. There's nothing here.
MAN:	They've … vanished.
WOMAN:	Do you think it's something we ate?

What does it mean in this initial scene to have real people playing historical individuals? Although Poppy's script does not name the Griffets, they are the woman, man, and son. As Freddie Rokem has pointed out, what makes theatrical representations of history different to other forms, such as the historical novel, is the 'live presence of the actors on stage'. They are not really the historical individuals, and the words they speak and actions they perform are not the ones that the Griffets spoke and performed. And yet their actions unfold in real time in front of the audience: they have a reality of their own. Something, nonetheless, is happening. For Rokem, the actors become 'hyper historians'. Not content merely to

---

[116] *Le Journal*, 21 June 1935.

describe or re-tell past events, they literally 'redo' them, 'reappearing' as someone 'that has actually existed in the past'. As 'hyper-historians', they become witnesses who re-present the past to an audience.[117] In the alternating scenes of her play about the Vichy case, Poppy uses a technique that crystallizes this function of actor-as-witness, the observer:

2.

POLICEMAN: I'd heard about them, before I first became involved with the family. Who hadn't heard about them? They were making life difficult for people. Bit of a change from the usual, they were. I mainly rode my horse around the gardens. Looking for petty thieves. Criminals who took advantage of tourists who came here for the Baths and to drink the waters. My wife works in the factory that bottles the fizzy water. They say if the Baths dry up, Vichy falls. Nearly everyone who lives here benefits from it. It was a pleasant summer. The city was thriving – a Tabac on every corner, golf courses, a casino. Picnics outside. Men in boaters taking ladies for a turn by the pergola.

They claimed their house was bewitched. They claimed they saw hundreds of them raining down. I always said there was something in the waters.

But I still kept drinking them.

Rokem points out that observers or eavesdroppers are key examples of how the characters on stage in performed histories become witnesses. The metatheatrical technique of presenting an audience on stage reminds the audience in the auditorium of the conceits of the history play. They are invited to identify with the observer on stage, but also to feel responsibility, and even shame or guilt, for the act of observing.[118] At the start of Poppy's script, the policeman is a detached observer whose scepticism contrasts with the mounting fears of the family in the other scenes:

3.

MAN: Are you seeing something?

WOMAN: Yes. Can you, son?

SON: Yes.

MAN: Everyone keep very still.

WOMAN: Hang on – what do you see?

SON: Needles. Like you use for sewing, Maman.

---

[117] Rokem, *Performing History*, 13, 25.   [118] Rokem, *Performing History*, pp.202-5

WOMAN: Hundreds of them?

SON: So many. Falling from the ceiling.

MAN: Impossible. We're indoors.

WOMAN: Perhaps there's a hole in the roof?

MAN: Earlier I found one in my café au lait.

The script here makes use of that foundational dynamic that Rokem identifies in histories performed on stage: something is happening, but it is not the real events of the past.

Our uncertainty about what is happening is also the uncertainty of the scene itself, which plays with materiality and perception. Will reflects after watching the scene performed:

> The needles have this brilliant theatrical power. We don't actually need real needles as props in order for the actors to stage finding them everywhere.
>
> They are so tiny that to an audience, them 'finding' needles might as well be them finding 'nothing'.
>
> The audience become complicit in the uncertainty.

As the script develops, and the family descend further into their own search for the elusive needles, the policeman's role shifts. Rather than the sceptical observer of his first monologues, his words become more bizarre and even, in Rokem's application of Tzvetlan Todorov's conception, fantastic.[119] Although the events clearly take place in the real world that the audience would recognize, the policeman starts to narrate incomprehensible transgressions of the normal rules of our reality:

4.

POLICEMAN: First, the waters dried up. That was after the first needles fell in the house. I remained vigilant, but the more involved I became with the family, the harder it was to doubt their story. I started to notice strange goings-on. Nobody was allowed to walk on the grass, unless barefoot. It rained every day for a week, but still no water came. Someone said that they saw the fountains spouting blood. Ladies starting wearing boaters and men felt more comfortable in dresses. It became impossible to lick stamps. People had to start treating their ailments with coffee. Refugees from Alsace wanted to come and see what the fuss was about, but we decided there was no work for them.

I begged everyone to stay in their homes.

But no-one listened.

---

[119] Rokem, *Performing History*, 36–7.

By the final monologue, the policeman's words mix factual details from Poppy's research into the context of Vichy in the 1930s with outlandish and nonsensical ideas:

6.

POLICEMAN: I'd been on the case for months. I practically lived with the family. I had to. Heavy snows made the roads impassable. Moustaches returned to their natural state as caterpillars and crawled under rocks. Everybody ran to the church, but it had been turned into a casino and was only admitting entry to cats. The synagogue was open, but required you to enter on skis, or with two golf clubs. There were bomb scares in seventeen locations, including schools. I had nausea. We all had nausea. A whole village near the city turned into cows. It was necessary to beat all the Priests. The Rabbis tried to help, so it became necessary to beat them too. Prisons overflowed with rosaries, which then had to be buried in the mud. People refused to eat eggs anymore, so the eggs rebelled. Bakers started to burn babies in their ovens, as a way to disinfect. Money no longer was relevant, because people were paying for everything with body parts. Women were advised to keep cheese between their breasts, and soon that was the only food left. Supplies stopped. No-one came in or out of the city. The people agreed to sacrifice themselves.

The needles kept falling, but only three people could see them.

In the alternating scenes of her script experiment drawing on the Vichy case, Poppy uses a technique that crystallizes the function of actor-as-witness, the observer. As her model for writing the Policeman's monologues, she began with Mrs Jarrett's dystopian monologues in Caryl Churchill's *Escaped Alone*.[120] However, unlike Mrs Jarrett's monologues in Churchill's play, which remain consistently fantastical, the Policeman's words grow more nonsensical with each monologue, to demonstrate how he becomes increasingly infected by the social contagion of witchcraft rumours.

The fantastical monologues express some of the humour in the original newspaper reporting of the case – a humour that was surprisingly common in court cases and newspaper reporting about witchcraft. But the fantastical elements also catch at the strangeness of the matter out of place that constitutes so many of the witchcraft cases. They translate the quotidian disturbances that such dislocations represent into dramatized examples so that we, the audience, can in some sense understand the magic that we are witness to.

---

[120] Caryl Churchill, *Escaped Alone* (London: Samuel French, 2020).

Such 'theatrical' techniques are not limited to playwriting. Any writing can be performed. And performance brings new understandings. When we rehearsed Anna's poems in a workshop with actors, we had different actors speak different lines of the pieces. They moved around the space as they spoke, miming actions that connected to the words they were speaking. The resulting poems were completely unlike the written originals. Anna picked up on how the staged poems became more than one single voice as the actors posed the questions in each piece to one another on stage or took different parts of the poem:

> The poem becomes more than just the one voice in my head, which is quite flat and meant to be read on the page. Working with Poppy and seeing how she writes scripts has encouraged me to think more about characters and different voices. Seeing the actors work with this poem revealed to me how a poem can have multiple perspectives within it. I mean that there could be different kinds of characters speaking within it – rather than just my voice on the page.
>
> Which is good isn't it? Especially if you're writing from history. Don't you want to be catching other kinds of voices?

4.7 Exercises

As with the other exercises in the Element, you should take some notes after doing the exercises. You may find it hard to take notes while you are doing them, so it can be a good idea to designate someone to be the 'director' and take notes throughout.

1. Improvise.
    a. For a warm-up, you could try this game that Robert Poynton learned from Keith Johnstone.[121] It's played in pairs. In each pair, one person mimes giving a gift to the other. They can pretend it is large or small, light or heavy, valuable or casual. The other person takes the gift and mimes opening it. They thank the gift-giver and describe what the gift is.
        i. The game is about discovering things in the present, and letting go of expectations ... but Poynton reminds readers that improv games like this don't have a 'point'. What do you find interesting about this game?
    b. Choose a real person from your research and try to improvise a scene where they have a conversation with another person.
        i. Prompts can be useful for this. It helps if the prompt each person is given brings them into conflict. You might tell one person they do not

---

[121] Robert Poynton, *Do Improvise: Less Push. More Pause. Better Results. A New Approach to Work (and Life)* (London: The Do Book Company, 2013), 33.

want to talk about a certain topic and tell the other to question them about that topic.

   ii. Objects are also useful. Can you choose props that reflect something about the person you have chosen? An item of clothing they might have owned, a book or picture, a piece of jewellery?

   iii. What surprised you in the improvisation? What new questions did you learn by trying to be your subject?

2. Actioning. Take a historical source that features dialogue, or a play script, and work out what each line is doing. What reaction does the person want to provoke in the other participants in the scene? Actions should be expressed as transitive verbs, things that people do *to* someone else.

   a. Try looking in Caladrone and Lloyd-Williams' *Actions: The Actors' Thesaurus* for examples.

   b. What do you learn from looking at a source or a scene like this? What surprises you? Do the actions suggest a story behind the story?

   c. Try doing this activity in a small group. Do you agree on actions for some lines? Which ones do you disagree on?

3. Dialogue your writing with a group. Take a piece of writing you have done or a primary source. This works well with poems and prose text, but can also be done with a script. It will need to be short: less than a page.

   a. Take it in turns to read through the pieces as a group. Do you see different possible voices in the writing? Discuss these with your group.

   b. Assign different people to read different parts as if they were dialogue. Try reading it through.

   c. Finally, 'block' the dialogue by having the different speakers use the physical space as well as the words they are reading.

   d. How does this change your understanding of the pieces?

5 Empathy

I sometimes think that good poets open themselves to all the voices in the air, and they are there, of the live and dead, of animal and plant and inert matter, of whatever inhabits the rest of the universe.[122]

We shouldn't condescend to the people of the past nor distort them into versions of ourselves.[123]

---

[122] Adam Plunkett, 'Talk to the Dead: An Interview with Alice Notley', 2015. https://www.poetry foundation.org/articles/141784/talk-to-the-dead.

[123] Hilary Mantel, 'The Iron Maiden', *The Reith Lectures*, 2017. https://bit.ly/3JCQTQn.

5.1 The Problem

Historians often encounter magic through hostile sources. It is easy to write accounts of magic in modern Europe that emphasize the deplorable 'survival' of superstitious beliefs, because this is what newspaper journalists, prosecutors, judges, and courtroom experts thought of magic. The challenge is to rediscover other perspectives: believers, of course, but also victims and bystanders. The range of possible attitudes to magic and witchcraft is much broader than reformers who deplored magic believed, as is the range of possible actors that we could consider. The blurring of distinctions between humans and others is one of the most commonly identified characteristics of magical 'worldviews'.[124] It is also an increasingly common methodological foundation for historians studying other living beings, and even the material cultures of the past.[125]

Empathy is a problem of method, but – perhaps more clearly than any other topic in this Element – it is also a problem of ethics. What right do we have to speak for the dead? What right do we even have to name people, and to label them as 'witches', or 'believers', or 'sceptics'? When dealing with the witchcraft cases, we are caught between two poles. On the one hand, our desire to give voice, as the poet Alice Notley does, to 'the live and dead' and even 'animal and plant and inert matter'. This is the project of historical recovery, the constant return to our sources to try to understand the silenced voices of the cases, to convey something of the experiences, emotions, and intentions of the actors involved. Do we not owe them this?

And yet.

The other pole of this dilemma is the difficulty, the audacity of empathy, and especially of a form of empathy that tries to understand not just other people but the many possible actors in a magical universe. By what right do we write? The poet Clare Shaw has written of the dangers of ventriloquism that borders on 'colonisation or theft'.[126] Would the people that we are writing about even want to be remembered? We have concerns about memorializing them through accounts of moments that may have been among the worst, most frightening, saddening, and shameful times in their lives. And how can we know if we are doing them justice? In a call to understand past subjectivities in their own terms, Lyndal Roper has argued that historians can be too quick to conclude any understanding is impossible. The result, she warns, is that the dead become our 'marionettes', dressed up in period costume such as 'ruffs and codpieces',

---

[124] A running theme in Gosden, *The History of Magic*.

[125] Emily O'Gorman and Andrea Gaynor, 'More-Than-Human Histories', *Environmental History* 25:4 (2020), 711–35.

[126] Clare Shaw, 'Gastromancy: Speaking from the Gut', 2016. https://poetryschool.com/theblog/gastromancy-speaking-gut/.

but fundamentally unable to 'surprise and unsettle'.[127] Historians often warn against 'condescending to' or 'distorting' the people of the past into what Hilary Mantel calls 'versions of ourselves'.[128] For the Australian historian Inga Clendinnen, empathy risked being too easy: misplaced and undisciplined, the instinctive identification that we might feel with individuals in the past can be a trap. For Clendinnen, the meticulous reconstitutive work of the historian was to be preferred to flashes of 'intuition'. We must, in Tom Griffith's summary of Clendinnen's views, 'work against the grain of empathy and intuition'.[129]

5.2 Change Perspective

We explore creative methods as a way to shake ourselves out of what Robert Darnton has called 'a false sense of familiarity with the past'.[130] Rather than identifying with the authorial voice in a newspaper story, for instance, we looked for other, submerged perspectives. We took the text of the article that appeared in *Le Journal* on 21 June 1935 describing the bewitchment of a family of grocers in Vichy (reproduced in translation in Section 4). We read the text quickly, listing all of the different perspectives implied in the text, from the bewitched grocers, to the unwitcher they called in, the priest, and the neighbours who witnessed the bewitchment.

But we also considered the non-human perspectives. Will writes:

> I was drawn to writing from the perspective of 'the whole region'. That perspective is evoked in the original newspaper story in a sentence that reads 'From that moment on, the whole region was convinced that they were victims of a witch!'

This is a strange way to think about belief, as if it belongs not to individuals but to a geography or a space. Using similar techniques to those described in Section 1, Will reorganized the text to speak in the voice of the 'region'. He explains:

> I thought it important to preserve whole phrases, to rub along the grain of the text as much as possible. The dashes between words and phrases mark the seams where I have rearranged the original text:
>
> I – contained – a veritable nest of – local know it alls – pranksters – police – pins – and – chickens. They would drag themselves around for a little bit, then all of a sudden – onto the roof of the house.

---

[127] Roper, *Oedipus and the Devil*, 11.

[128] Mantel, 'The Iron Maiden'. See, for example, the discussion in Robert Darnton, *The Great Cat Massacre and Other Episodes in French Cultural History* (New York: Vintage Books, 1985), 12.

[129] Tom Griffiths, *The Art of Time Travel: Historians and Their Craft* (Victoria: Schwartz Publishing, 2016), 260–4.

[130] Darnton, *The Great Cat Massacre*, 4.

I – contained – the Boutiron bridge – the outskirts of Vichy – next to that – a large heart, drawn in chalk, and stuck all over with pins. I – was – a sealed envelope – bristling with needles – nothing out of the ordinary – the priest – immediately agreed.

I – contained – the reputation of – peace until one day – they found a – slaughter – survivors – the Spa Company – 27 chickens! Their heads swelled up and turned red, and blood came from their – everywhere – inside the house – the chicken coop – under a plank near the door.

I – was convinced that they were victims of a witch!

The rearrangement of the words emphasizes the perspective of place itself: it focuses on insides and outsides, houses and villages, envelopes and piercings. Witchcraft becomes a question of what Mary Douglas called 'matter out of place': dirt, and the transgression of boundaries.[131] The reconstituted text is linked together in a chain which comments on the original claim in the newspaper story. In a sense, the region here does 'believe' they were victims of a witch, but only if we accept that belief can be stitched together, discontinuous, and inconsistent. In choosing to re-tell the story from the perspective of the region, the cut-up also highlights something about the original text: in one short phrase, the 'region' expresses a clearer opinion, agency, and subjectivity than most of the human participants in the case.

Any given text implies a multitude of such unexpected perspectives. Will writes:

> I was also drawn to the animals in the case. Their deaths are what first arouses suspicions of witchcraft, but as so often in similar cases, their perspective is absent from the newspaper account. How could I re-tell the same story, use the same words to hear the chickens?
>
> I cut the text up, using a sharp tool, like a chicken might scratch it apart, pecking it into small pieces. I focus on the things that might interest a chicken.
>
> I place the pieces on the page in short bursts and longer streams to capture the sometimes-spasmodic movements of a chicken, the way that they move in bursts, pausing with a kind of ponderousness, before darting in a new direction. I think this also gives the text a much darker feel than the original news story. Seeing things from the chicken's point of view is – perhaps unsurprisingly – much more violent, desperate, and scared.

Cases of inexplicable material phenomena such as the Vichy case, or the 1861 case in Lyon discussed above, pull our attention from people to animals and things. Anna was struck by the phrase that the *Journal de*

---

[131] Mary Douglas, *Purity and Danger: An Analysis of Concepts of Pollution and Taboo* (London: Routledge, 1966). On witchcraft as 'matter out of place', see Purkiss, *The Witch in History*, 119–44.

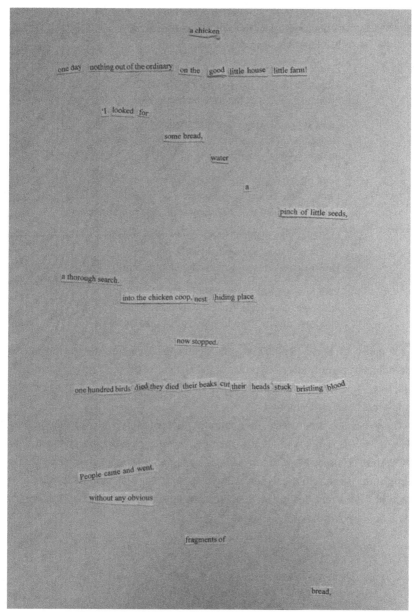

Figure 3 Will's poem 'A Chicken'

Toulouse of 23 December 1861 used to describe these mysterious events: 'Missiles fall from the ceiling, thrown by invisible hands.' Her poem 'Invisible Hands' is a meditation on the confusion of agencies in the case:

The loom is my monster-mistress.
A big-headed Madame with snake tresses.
I feed her silk, she calls me little worm.

Like a garden after rain, the whole quartier
squirms with girls like me, easy to squish.
I pink and deafen as Madame boxes my ears.

Tears are not worthy of my time. Instead my
stopped-whimper is a missile: I rain down
bobbins, stones yanked from these walls.

Send for the doctor, the sorcerer, the secret police.
I'm invisible as a grub or a goddess or a curse.
Magic is real action. I will deny it all. A gob of spittle

bullseyes your stubbled cheek. How many worms
does it take to weave a witch, a ghost, a devil.
How many worms to weave a dream of escape.

I am Mélanie and Marie. Your history is riddled
with holes I've made. Cut me in two and I split
direction, mutate. I am laughing girls, running away.

Like many of these perspective pieces, the poem addresses its own subjectivity. It is not just from the point of view of the 'little worm', or Mélanie, or Marie, but about the impossibility of that point of view, the holes that riddle the history.

Cows became a particular fascination. Often a family's most valuable possession, perhaps a loved family member, cows have long been central to witchcraft accusations as victims of milk-magic, and butter that inexplicably turns sour. Anna wrote cows by applying the erasure techniques explored in Section 3 to a text dealing with curses placed on cows from *Le Folklore du Dauphiné* by Arnold Van Gennep:[132]

cows impossible milk

            cows bewitched milk
            impossible neighbours

                        out udder   butter
                        out house   neighbours

What might be gained by a cow speaking?

Wittgenstein famously said that if a lion could speak we wouldn't be able to understand him. This is because we share no common worldly references with a

---
[132] Arnold van Gennep, *Le folklore du Dauphiné (Isère)* (Paris: Librairie orientale et américaine, 1932).

lion – we live in completely different perceptual realms. Surely this is the same for the cow? Or is it? Could the cow help us understand and articulate more fully what witchcraft cases mean to human participants, too?

For the following extract from a scene, Poppy researched 1920s farming practices and mastitis in cow udders to write about a case of bewitched cows from the Morbihan in 1920:

Barbra moves around Louis' garden, grabbing flowers and eating them.

Louis: Monsieur Chevrolet! She's at it again!

She looks at him.

She licks her knee.

He claps his hands and walks towards her.

Louis: Back! Get away from me! Shoo!

He stops.

Barbra: It hurts. It hurts. Swelling. I can run from you. Heat. Hardness. Pain. It's so hot, do you feel hot, I feel hot, god, it's hot out here. I'm thirsty. It hurts. I shit myself all the time.

The scene plays on audience expectations about perspective. A human actor playing Barbra behaves bizarrely, almost incomprehensively. It is not until Barbra speaks that she gives the game away.

In 2018, Laura Gustafsson and Terike Haapoja curated an exhibition on 'History According to Cattle'. In the essay accompanying the exhibition, they write:

> Expressing the viewpoint of an animal in a work of art can, if not bridge, then at least question the gap between us and the Other, whilst at the same time embracing an acceptance of the deficiencies inherent to the chosen methodology. Art is self-reflexive, invariably exposing the inherent subjectivity of its chosen medium. Whenever art says something, it simultaneously questions what is being said and how it is said. Art even uses language to expose its own limitations, quietly making space for what is normally excluded from the linguistic realm.[133]

Magic is by nature hard to pin down. It is what happens when uncertainty creeps into our understanding of agency. Or perhaps it is when agency means something much more encompassing than our often-anthropocentric points of view. We seek a diversity of possible perspectives, not because we can prove

---

[133] Laura Gustafsson and Terike Haapoja, 'Imagining Non-human Realities', in *History According to Cattle* (Baltimore, MD: Project Muse, 2020), 109.

what a cow, a chicken, or a cupboard 'feels' or 'thinks', but for the sake of holding that multiplicity in mind when we think about witchcraft.

5.3 Case Study 7: Paris, 1877

The following story appeared in the newspaper *La Lanterne* on 26 September 1877. This anticlerical newspaper was particularly critical of the government of 'moral order' in the 1870s. Although France remained a republic, President MacMahon made no secret of his attachment to the royalist cause and the defence of 'Catholic' values. Anticlerical newspapers such as *La Lanterne* used stories of what they called 'superstition' to criticize this government for its conservatism:

> Could the moral order be taking us back to the good old days of superstition?
>
> Yesterday, on rue Violet, a considerable gathering could be found outside the fruit merchants run by the B ..., at no. 33.
>
> Having been informed of this gathering, the police superintendent visited the premises and questioned the fruit merchant as to what could have brought so many people to his establishment. M. B ... and his wife told the officer that witches had installed themselves in their cupboard, and that, not content with taking a small case of valuables, had amused themselves by breaking their crockery during the night. The superintendent initially thought the couple must be mad, but was soon convinced that the B ... were reporting these facts in good faith.
>
> These good people are rather gullible and would, had not various individuals intervened, have gone to the Church to find a priest to come and exorcise the evil spirits.
>
> Perhaps the real evil spirits were the neighbours making fun of M. and Mme B ... 's credulity.

We want to read between the lines of this sarcastic text, to empathize with the perspectives that are dismissed by the journalist: the crowd, the grocers, perhaps even the cupboard itself. How can we reanimate the magic of the case? By multiplying our metaphors for this work of empathy: it is a haunting, a channelling, an amplification, a scrying.

5.4 Make Methods of Metaphors

To work with the dead is to be haunted. The historian knows that this is impossible: the dead do not come back. The creative practitioner is not so sure.

'What, has this thing appeared again tonight?'

Freddie Rokem suggests that this question, which Marcellus asks in *Hamlet*, condenses the general relationship between theatrical performance and the historical past. Rokem argues that the question:

implies that the repressed ghostly figures and events from that ('real') historical past can (re)appear on the stage in theatrical performances. The actors performing such historical figures are in fact the 'things' who are appearing again tonight in the performance. And when these ghosts are historical figures they are in a sense performing history.[134]

All stages, Marvin Carlson argues, are haunted.[135] Haunted by past performances, by other actors, by events, by the past.

Many other metaphors of this haunting focus on sound and voice. Saidiya Hartman, for instance, writes of 'amplifying' the sources she worked with.[136] Others focus on other senses. Many historians think of their work as textural. Documents, we are taught, have a 'grain'. We read 'against' it, or along it.[137] We feel our sources. Will reflects:

> But if historians routinely make methods of metaphors, we could do better at making this metaphorical work visible. After working with Anna and Poppy I find myself thinking about how historical writing often submerges its own metaphorical methods, or alludes to widely held metaphors of historical writing, research, and historical events.

Creative writers have been more open about how metaphors do real work. The verbatim playwright Anna Deavere Smith discusses the power of repeating the words of others as a kind of possession: 'My grandfather told me that if you say a word often enough, it becomes you. ... manipulating words has a spiritual power'. Smith's creative technique is to listen to voice recordings of interviewees to learn to perfectly mimic their speech patterns. This is voicing the other at its purest:

> You listen to some of the characters and you begin to identify with them. Because I'm saying the stuff over and over again every night, part of me is becoming them through repetition – by doing the performance of themselves that they do.[138]

The poet Alice Notley and the historian Saidiya Hartman have described a similar erasure of the self that comes from voicing the other. Notley says:

> I am bombarded constantly by other voices when I sit down to write. I kind of don't have a self now, it's a rote thing, but I seem to hear what everyone else is

---

[134] Rokem, *Performing History*, 6.

[135] Marvin Carlson, *The Haunted Stage: The Theatre as Memory Machine* (Ann Arbor: University of Michigan Press, 2003).

[136] Hartman, *Wayward Lives*, xv.

[137] Ann Laura Stoler, *Along the Archival Grain: Epistemic Anxieties and Colonial Common Sense* (Princeton, NJ: Princeton University Press, 2009).

[138] Anna Deavere Smith and Carol Martin, 'The Word Becomes You: An Interview', *The Drama Review* 37:4 (1993), 45–62, 51, 57.

saying, particularly the dead … I'm never sure whether I'm really hearing other voices or am inhabiting my imagination. … I am obviously walking some line between charlatanism and authenticity that is scary and satisfying.[139]

For Hartman, recreating 'the voices and words' of her subjects required what she calls 'a mode of close narration, a style which places the voice of the narrator and character in inseparable relation, so that the vision, language, and rhythms of the wayward shape and arrange the text'.[140]

We use the techniques of monologue to similar effect: we try to speak 'as' the different perspectives in the cases. We are in dangerous territory. How can we know when we are channelling the voices of the dead, and when we are just hearing voices? Anna describes her understanding of this process: it is something like the techniques of scrying described in some of the witchcraft cases. In 1829, for instance, a man in Champtocé was promised he would see the image of a 'witch' in a jug of water. He recognized his brother-in-law, whom he then murdered.[141] Anna reflects:

> I *wish* there to be authenticity in the voices of the others I've written. Like scrying, I think the creative work maintains eye contact with the sources, but is a through-the-looking-glass version of history. The act of scrying reflects the viewer's own dark feelings back at them.

Cases which involved scrying, such as the Champtocé murder, are a caution for us. To what extent does the viewer see who they want to see in the reflection? The magic of scrying may simply be to make us aware of how we already feel about a person, to reflect our own expectations back at us.

Again, it can be an advantage to choose the impossible perspective. In a monologue poem about the 1877 haunted Parisian cupboard, Anna speaks in the voice of the cupboard itself. She reflects:

> I consider the emotion of the case – what feels to me like its *distress*. Sited inside the cupboard, there is something supernatural, disruptive, and painful. As a container and/or a void, the cupboard is an irresistible metaphor for the interior self in the following extract from the poem:

I am every shattering feeling you imagine　　or try not to　　imagine I am a crystal-quality shape-shifter　　I am a jar smashing　a blood-black　spill

a turbulence of voices – tongue-on-a-platter bowl-smasher

　　　　　　　　　　　　　broken pieces tumble out of me

---

[139] Plunkett, 'Talk to the Dead'.　　[140] Hartman, *Wayward Lives*, xiv.
[141] *Gazette des Tribunaux*, 16 November 1829.

Cupboards cannot literally speak. But consider how much factual research is involved in imagining the perspective of a cupboard. Anna writes:

> To get close to the cupboard, I wanted to know what it contained (other than sadness and a witch). I find vintage images of sardine tins, which enter my poem as *salted sardine tears*.

Piecing together this factual material allows Anna's poem to explore the case through metaphor. She suggests that:

> The poem looks like a cupboard. It looks like a squarish brown cupboard. A messy cupboard kept by a bad housewife. It's full of tins and crockery and thoughts someone wanted to hide in a hurry.
> The work is black words on a white page, arranged in a squarish shape. No punctuation but a smattering of capitals. Some deliberate gaps in the blocky text to indicate the struggle for voice.

The poem expresses feelings in motion. Everything is 'shattering', 'shifting', 'smashing', 'spilled', 'broken' and 'tumbling' in 'turbulence'. It is one example of a way to unpack what is dissonant and uncertain within witchcraft cases, and in our relations to them. Exploring these emotions reaches towards the unknowability of witchcraft, rather than trying to reduce it to alternate explanations. The metaphorical 'speaking' for the cupboard becomes a tool to help us think about the meanings magic held.

Another case that took place in Bordeaux in the same year as the haunted grocers' cupboard encourages us to think even more closely about objects.

5.5 Case Study 8: Bordeaux, 1877

The following story appeared in *La Petite Gironde* on 23 November 1877:

> On the rue des Terres-de-Bordes live a respectable family, father, mother, and five children. The father works in town, the mother sells coffee, and the children are growing by the day. The whole lot live in peace. But for a month, appalling things have been going on: every morning, the doorstep of the café is covered in salt, cooking salt. And every morning, the local gossips come to see the *mystery* and to pass comment, accompanied by many signs of the cross. Some go as far as saying the words of the exorcism aloud. – Don't laugh, dear reader. – These are deplorable developments. Sorcerology informs us that if you sow salt, you will grow witches. In fact, they are growing so well that anyone visiting the café last week would see that the clientele have abandoned it, and left a vacuum around the house.
> The mysteries take place each night, during the witching hour, when shadow-dark devils rush to the call of demonologists, drying up the church fonts, knocking over the *prie-Dieus*, upturning the prayer books and gagging the guardian angels, some of whom fall asleep.

You can see why such goings-on mean that the folk of the Terres-des-Bordes have put a red mark against the cursed household.

If the guardian angels are losing the Latin from their hymn books, then the police – who may not be angels, but are at least guardians – should put an end to these reprehensible bewitchments.

Here is a respectable woman whose clients have abandoned her because salt is being spread on her doorstep at night. This practice, wherever it originates, is clearly harming the interests of this poor mother, and is therefore a crime.

The police are obliged to intervene. Better than anyone else, they can conjure this spell: nothing cures witchcraft like a prison sentence.

Like the case in Paris the same year, the newspaper account of the disturbance in Bordeaux is framed by the disdain and scepticism of the journalist. And like the haunted grocers' cupboard, the mystery in Bordeaux is a mystery of matter. There is no explanation of the supposed witchcraft in the newspaper story: there is only the fact of the salt itself. What can we do with the often-stubborn mute materiality of cases like this?

5.6 Use Props

We work to use objects as a route into empathy.

Anna wrote several poems based on the Vichy case, including 'Premonition, 1935', a poem focusing on the needles in the case. The needles remind her of what Laura Maiklem has written about mudlarking and her favourite finds:

> My favourite kinds of treasures are pins, because there is nothing more ordinary than a pin. When I pick up a pin I think of the hands that touched it, the pincushion it was pulled from the morning it was lost, the clothes it held together and the conversations that were had while it was being worn. So many lives have touched each pin … Pins are not like precious jewels, they weren't loved or looked after, they were just part of everyday life.[142]

Anna reflects on how the needles in the Vichy case are similar:

> As a familiar, everyday object, they work as a route into empathy. It's easy to picture them, almost to *feel* them. Reading about them multiplied and out of place, it's unsettling:

> > Needles are raining from the sky
> > in Vichy, 1935. Look down my telescope
> > and survey the edge-lands they are living on.
> > A cusp, a dusk. Clouds swelling with metal.

---

[142] Lara Maiklem, *Mudlarking: Lost and Found on the River Thames* (London: Bloomsbury, 2019), 86.

Alarm bells sound in Vichy, 1935. No telescope
views their future but what they taste is mouthfuls
of metal in clouds of butter. Dusk spits pins.
Neighbours sweep needles from the gutter.

A taste of the future is mouthfuls of bullets.
Pick a needle from your morning *café au lait*.
Sweep neighbours into the gutter. Needles
are contagious like you can get used to anything.

Stir your morning milky coffee, sugar it with needles.
Survey the lie of your land. Are you living on the edge yet?
You could get to like it. Premonitions. Contagions.
Needles raining from the sky.

The suspension of disbelief in theatre depends on objects. On stage, a chair can become a little girl.[143] The audience co-creates by bringing their will to imagine into the room. As the artist Michael Craig-Martin has put it:

> belief underlies our whole experience of art. You either believe in a work or you do not. If you engage with a work, it can become magical, and if you do not, nothing happens, no matter how great the work itself.[144]

What happens in performed histories about the witchcraft cases comes close to what the people involved believed was happening. Objects play a special role in this process: they stand for the remains of magical practice or a materialization of witchcraft itself. Sorcery might be unseen, but it makes use of things – in sympathetic magic, to lay and to ward off curses. The objects may not be the magic, but they are its materiality. When we want to feel things about witchcraft, we feel the things of witchcraft. To supplement the textual nature of our sources, we seek the visual: we explore online, ask what people's clothes, homes, workplaces, streets looked like in the past. In museum collections, we encounter the objects of our historical sources, in three dimensions: here is a milk churn, a toad stuck with thorns, a 100-year-old potato carried to heal rheumatism, an ancient bottle of urine.

How can these things help us think about witchcraft? We are not engaged in literal archaeology, a discipline with its own methods, conventions, and questions. We are not interested in the techniques of analysing objects for age or composition. Instead, we are interested in the creative use of objects. Just as ordinary objects are repurposed for witchcraft, so as writers and performers we repurpose the objects we find in our sources, in our museums, in online images,

---

[143] Tim Crouch, *An Oak Tree* (London: Oberon Books, 2015).
[144] Michael Craig-Martin, *On Being an Artist* (London: Art Books Publishing, 2015), 132.

and employ them to add detail, veracity, and texture to our writing. We re-create them to add vitality and context, and to wonder about them.

We look for props. A poet invited to work with us as a guest collaborator, E. E. Nobbs, describes the process of thinking about the objects in an 1877 case of a bewitched cupboard in Paris:

> Looking for a hook, I check out the definition of 'crockery', which leads me to 'crock' as a storage vessel. I track down European companies which produced earthenware in the second half of the nineteenth century. I follow the trail to images of vintage mustard crocks on eBay, and these items become the focus of my poem 'After the Exorcism'.[145]

Such objects are always already symbolic. Having noticed that salt is mentioned in many of the cases, Poppy decided to focus on the 1877 Bordeaux case, with its unexpected salt:

> I wrote several short scenes that put the *salt* centre stage. In the following draft, the amount of salt on the doorstep keeps on increasing, beyond what is realistic, until the scene climaxes:
>
> *A cascade of salt pours out of the door, knocking the man off the step.*
>
> Man: Aidez-moi! Le sel!
>
> *He is covered in salt, but manages to light a cigarette.*
> *The woman comes out of the house.*
> *She takes the cigarette out his mouth, and extinguishes it in the salt.*

Poppy reflects:

> Really, this would be nearly impossible to stage! But what it dramatises, via the objects, the salt, is the swamping dread of being afraid, of feeling victimised, or bewitched. How witchcraft fears overwhelm, drown and bury. How salt can strangle.

Another object-based technique that we used when working with actors and modern pagans was 'character boxes'. We made up four boxes with objects that were related to the lives of four individuals we were interested in. We did not give the actors or pagans any further information about the 'characters', simply leaving the participants to interpret the objects themselves. We made a box for a man named Joseph who killed a neighbour who he thought was a witch. We put a hunting knife handbook for rural constables in the box, as he was a *garde-champêtre*, or type of game-keeper. We also included a crucifix, because he had been advised by healers and local monks to use crucifixes to protect himself. A picture of a pageant day in Alsace in the 1920s gave an idea of what the village

---

[145] https://creativewitchcraft.wordpress.com/guest-poets/.

where he lived might have looked like around the Easter celebrations when he killed his victim. Another box related to a fortune-teller and unwitcher named 'Madame Flora', whose practices were described by the anthropologist Jeanne Favret-Saada in the 1970s.[146] In the box we put a set of the Lenormand Tarot cards that Madame Flora used, along with some more speculative items. Anna wondered if Madame Flora might drink crème de cassis. Will suggested a pendant of the Virgin Mary and a vial of holy water, as many practitioners of this kind often made use of Catholic devotional items.

The objects acted as a bridge between our knowledge of these individuals and the other participants' assumptions. One of the actors, Joanna Cross, reflected:

> The artefact boxes were essential to building belief into context and character. Before an improvisation, I was briefed about how volatile the character Joseph could be. Without premeditation I went straight over to the Joseph box, took out the hunting knife, and hid it. Somehow that artefact had already, and in a short space of time, contributed to my engagement with the situation.

Another actor, Alan Coveney, talked in general about the importance of these character boxes to how the rehearsals developed:

> It was a brilliant way to get our imaginations working but in a very focused way. Actors invariably respond better to objects rather than concepts, and the variety of materials – photos, historical documents, domestic implements, weapons even – not only created a sense of excitement and discovery but catapulted us into the lives of the characters and made an imaginary social and emotional world much more tangible.

We are rarely able to actually touch objects connected to the historical cases: judicial archives preserve paper records but seldom material evidence. But in this exercise, the objects we use stand in for the real thing. They act as props. As long as we behave as if we believe in them, they mediate a relationship to the past that did not just pass through words. They allow the actors to perform versions of the past that are something more than just our interpretations of what the sources say.

5.7 Exercises

Take notes after you have done each exercise. Think of these notes and the exercises themselves as a research process.

1. Character cut ups: take a textual primary source. This works well with a source of between 200 and 1,000 words.

---

[146] Jeanne Favret-Saada, *The Anti-witch*, trans. Matthew Carey (Chicago, IL: Hau Books, 2009), 47–80.

   a. Read through the source once, listing as many perspectives as you can within the source. Interpret 'perspective' as broadly or as narrowly as you like. The more options you have, the better.

   b. Look at your list of perspectives and choose the one that most surprises you. Choose one that would not have occurred to you before you drew up the list.

   c. Give yourself fifteen minutes to cut up the text and produce a monologue that speaks in the voice of this perspective. You can cut the text up electronically, using a word processor, or try using scissors or a craft knife on a printout. Come up with your own rules, appropriate to the perspective you want to write. How will you cut the text up? How will you rearrange it on the page?

   d. This exercise works especially well if you do it several times with the same text, working on different perspectives using the same starting point.

2. Develop new metaphors for empathy.

   a. Try free-writing about how you think about giving voice to historical subjects.

   b. Are there any surprises? Are there images or ideas about empathy that you had not considered before? Does your subject material contain metaphors for empathy you had not considered before?

   c. Put a timer on for five minutes. Free-write a monologue from a character's perspective. You could choose an object, a place, an animal, and not just a human perspective.

      i. Which metaphors best suit your ways of empathizing with this perspective? Try sensory metaphors, but try to think of other ways to think about empathy, too.

3. Character boxes. For this group exercise you should each choose one historical character you are interested in. Don't tell the other people in the group ahead of time who you have chosen.

   a. The first stage is making your box.

      i. What objects do you know they used or owned? Look for similar objects to include in the box.

      ii. If you like, you can also be more speculative, like the crème de cassis we put in Madame Flora's box.

   b. The next stage involves sharing the boxes and improvising from them.

      i. Explore the contents of each box in turn. The person who made the box should not say anything before it is opened. You may want to allow them to answer questions about the objects or the person, but it can be rewarding to let people guess, without confirming anything.

Spend at least ten minutes on each box. The more you do, the more rewarding this will be.

ii. After the group has explored all of the boxes, assign one person to be the character represented by each box. Put yourself into pairs and talk about who you think your character is with your partner.

iii. What would happen if your two characters met? Discuss the possibilities with your partner and, when you have settled on one, try improvising a short scene.

iv. Another person should act as director for each scene. Your job is to encourage the two characters without interrupting what they are doing. When you think the scene has reached a natural conclusion, you can clap.

4. Emotional props. This group exercise works well with a museum, but you could do it with any collection of objects.

a. Have each person write as many objects as they remember from the museum, each on a separate piece of paper. Make a pile of all of these pieces of paper together. Keep it separate from the pieces of paper for the next stage.

b. Now have each person write the emotions or feelings they had when they saw the objects, also on separate pieces of paper. Make all of these scraps of paper with feelings into a new pile.

c. Each person then takes an object and a feeling and writes for between one and three minutes, using the format: X object made me feel Y, because…

d. Which of these was hardest? Why was it hard to pretend to feel that?

6 Epilogue

Creative research methods are radically different to many of the research methods inspired by social science that have influenced the academic study of magic. They do not necessarily start with clear questions or provide definitive answers at the end of the process. This very indeterminacy is what makes them so well-suited to the study of magic. For Diane Purkiss, the 'witch' is by nature impossible to define, and academic efforts to do so are just one more example of how this figure has been reconstructed in 'conflict and contestation between diverse groups', from the early modern trials through to neo-pagans today.[147]

---

[147] Purkiss, *The Witch in History*, 2–4, 93.

In approaching witchcraft through creative practice, we have sought to preserve some of this indeterminacy, to leave some of the gaps unfilled. Like Donna Haraway, we have tried to 'stay with the trouble'.[148]

This is emotional work. Poppy reflects that:

> Often, in life, academia, and our creative practice, we praise and empower and applaud. Sometimes we leave little room to critique, to challenge and acknowledge our bad feelings.
>
> Witchcraft is trouble. It stirs things up, and the people in our cases often wanted a quick, protective fix from it – from stopping an imagined future happening. Theatre is also trouble. For exactly the same reasons.
>
> It seems inherently wrong to use the worst moment in someone's life as a catalyst for creative writing. Why must these moments of burning, defrauding, and violence be all that is remembered?
>
> When I write scenes, do I turn real people's actual bad feelings into something that is kitsch and digestible for a contemporary audience? How do I feel about doing that?

But it is also intellectual work.

Staying with the trouble in this context means not resolving the problems or questions that the cases raise: was Madame A. really 'delusional'? Were her neighbours casting spells on her and her husband? The interest of these stories is not in answering the questions that were so important to newspaper reports of the case, the police, the criminal trial, or the medical experts called to give evidence. Staying with the trouble is about taking the measure of these mysteries, probing their shapes and meanings, their resonances and silences.

Staying with the trouble means slowing down. We slow down to focus not just on close readings of the primary sources from the research, but to do more close writing, to get between the lines of the sources. In cases where what was always at stake was the very nature of what was possible, we probe uncertainty to emphasize the sensory and material thickness of stories, to take flashes or moments seriously. This kind of work appeals beyond academia. Describing Anna's prize-winning poem 'Holy Cow' from the project, the poet Patience Agbabi writes:

> I admire the boldness of it, the directness, 'she moos'; the use of vernacular 'I've the mother of a backache'; the similes, the metaphors, each word carefully chosen; the musicality of the form – tercets with medium-long-medium lines; the subtle consonance and assonance.[149]

---

[148] Donna Haraway, *Staying with the Trouble: Making Kin in the Cthulucene* (Durham, NC: Duke University Press, 2016).

[149] See: www.writeoutloud.net/public/blogentry.php?blogentryid=94017.

Close writing like this helps us to develop a plural, flexible, and sharpened historical imagination. This is imagination that is not only outright fabulation or pure invention, but also the imaginative work of collage, assembly, and presentation which even non-fiction writers engage in.

Only this kind of imagination allows us to identify with and understand the viewpoints submerged in historical sources: not just the sceptical outsiders, but believers, perhaps even 'witches' themselves, or the many other beings and things involved in witchcraft, from cows and chickens to cupboards and crockery. Judicial records and newspaper accounts present a relentlessly negative view of the people who feared witches as credulous and naïve, emphasizing rural isolation, poverty, and poor education as the root causes of the fear of witches. Anna reflected:

> One of the things that struck me was how tidy the newspaper stories are. They are written to sew things up or to titillate, or to mock.

Historians might be accustomed to thinking of this as source bias, but creative practices offer other ways to frame this homogeneity. The writer Chimamanda Ngozi Adichie, for instance, has talked of the danger of a single story: 'The single story creates stereotypes, and the problem with stereotypes is not that they are untrue, but they are incomplete. They make one story become the only story'.[150] Anna remembers:

> I begin to think that this witch of dark feelings abjected, or female power celebrated, lives on the *inside*, she has been with us for so long.

Poppy notes:

> Many plays I've read feature the accused female 'witch' as a central character. The women who were abused, hounded, and murdered out of history have – in some small way – been given their voice back. This is necessary work. Clearly, in the early modern period, women were especially targeted, accused, and horrifically murdered – that is of course a vital story to tell, but it is now one that has been produced a lot across different mediums.

Will agrees:

> Accused witches – especially women – have been central to creative work addressing the histories of witchcraft. Artists and writers are drawn to the drama of the well-known early modern trials. But it is as if the only thing relevant to modern societies about witchcraft beliefs has become that

---

[150] Chimamanda Ngozi Adichie, 'The Danger of a Single Story', 2009. https://bit.ly/3KGrx4b.

experience of unjust persecution and its links to our own ideas about femininity today.

What else might there be to say?

We have sought – in the words of Adichie – to 'balance' the stories. Focusing closely on the nineteenth- and twentieth-century French sources, we try to tell less-heard stories of suspected and accused witches. Stories that satisfy curiosity about the witch but complicate the myth and pay attention to detail. We open up the story by writing from the perspective of a murderer, a cursed cow, a bewitched cupboard, a commercial witch, a woman judged delusional. We do not just find women falsely accused of witchcraft, but a set of associations of men, violence, and magic, and a range of everyday magical objects, such as bobbins and needles, and modern objects, such as cars or a 'radioactive pen'.

At times, we have been microhistorians: an individual case can be a kind of 'normal exception' that allows us to imagine what we can never know about hundreds of other cases where the documentation is much slimmer.[151] But we proved too greedy to be true microhistorians. Or perhaps too promiscuous. Instead of the individual case study, we become pointillists, collectors of miniatures. Rather than telling one big story, our project has become to tell many specific stories. We do not synthesize, we accumulate. As poets, we seek thingness and detail. As historians, we undercut stereotypes with the idiosyncrasies of multitude. We have, at times, rejected narrative completely; presented dramatic moments, an image, broken-off thoughts.

Most academic research is turned into journal articles, book chapters, books, or perhaps blogs or opinion pieces. But these forms are not always the forms that speak most easily to audiences who may be interested in this research. There is a broad interest in magic today, noted by researchers and journalists, and expressed through social media such as TikTok, Instagram, Facebook, and Twitter. Poetry and other forms of creative writing can act as bridges between newer social media and more traditional publishing formats, and as a key location of discussions of the imaginative and spiritual salvage of historical magic.[152] During the creative witches project, theatre, improvisation, and poetry writing provided ways for Anna, Poppy, and Will to work with contemporary pagans on their understandings of the histories of magic. It can be challenging to include the

---

[151] Edward Muir, 'Observing Trifles', in *Microhistory and the Lost Peoples of Europe*, Edward Muir and Guido Ruggieri (eds.) (Baltimore: Johns Hopkins University Press, 1991).

[152] For example: Sarah Shin and Rebecca Tamás (eds.), *Spells: 21st century Occult Poetry* (Ignota, 2018).

perspectives and interests of pagans in academic historical writing about magic, because of differing epistemologies and historical metanarratives. Working creatively with our pagan collaborators provided a way instead to suspend potential differences and imagine, together.

A turn to creative forms has also been a way to recognize just how much history is being done by poets, theatre-makers, and other creative practitioners, particularly since the growth of what David Shields has called 'reality hunger' among artists and writers.[153] As the playwright on the project, Poppy encouraged us to explore the techniques of what Carol Martin has grouped together as 'theatre of the real'. Different forms, including docudrama, documentary theatre, verbatim theatre, tribunal theatre, and theatre of fact all draw from real history, and place real people on stage using different dramaturgical methods.[154] This theatre of the real may only be loosely based on real events, or the entire script may be edited from real-life words spoken during interviews or court-hearings. Theatre overlaps here with historiography, as Freddie Rokem has noted:

> Theatre performing history partially takes over the role of the professional historian. But the means used by the theatre are indeed very different from those used by academic historiographers.[155]

In a similar way, Anna drew on the long tradition of poetry as history as a means to memorialize and render select historical events memorable. As Ted Hughes has argued, poetry can work to bring the past 'near and real' – it can deliver us history on a human scale.[156] In recent years, a poetic turn to history has been driven by an ethics of un-forgetting, of telling the unofficial story, asserting marginalized identities, and documenting lesser-heard stories of racism, colonialism, sexism, and homophobia. Poets like Jay Bernard, Hannah Lowe, and Tara Bergin work from the archive to write intimate, imagined stories from real sources.[157] Others, such as Robin Coste Lewis and Susan Howe, challenge the historical record by using found historical text.[158] Within the context of histories of witchcraft, poetry can provide proximity to the experiences of workers, 'peasants',

---

[153] David Shields, *Reality Hunger: A Manifesto* (New York: Knopf, 2010). On theatre, see Alison Forsyth and Chris Megson, *Get Real: Documentary Theatre Past and Present* (Basingstoke: Palgrave Macmillan, 2009).

[154] Carol Martin, *Theatre of the Real* (Basingstoke: Palgrave Macmillan, 2015).

[155] Rokem, *Performing History*, p.24.   [156] Hughes, *Poetry in the Making*, p.43.

[157] Jay Bernard *Surge* (London: Chatto and Windus, 2019); Tara Bergin *The Tragic Death of Eleanor Marx* (Manchester: Carcanet Press, 2017); Lowe, *Ormonde*.

[158] Robin Coste Lewis, *Voyage of the Sable Venus and Other Poems* (New York: Knopf, 2020); Susan Howe, *That This* (New York: New Directions, 2010).

and the 'delusional'. It can get 'near and real' to experiences of fear, doubt, and belief in which the boundaries between imagination and reality are indistinct.

Poets and playwrights are already making histories of magic like this.

Academics who want to join those conversations and engage with other researchers and audiences will have to consider meeting these other practices of history halfway.

References

Academy of American Poets, 'Haiku'. https://poets.org/glossary/haiku.

Adichie, Chimamanda Ngozi, 'The Danger of a Single Story', Ted Talk, 2009. https://bit.ly/3KGrx4b.

Ankarloo, Bengt and Stuart Clark (eds.), *Witchcraft and Magic in Europe: The Eighteenth and Nineteenth Centuries* (Philadelphia: University of Pennsylvania Press, 1999).

Bergin, Tara, *The Tragic Death of Eleanor Marx* (Manchester: Carcanet Press, 2017).

Bernard, Jay, *Surge* (London: Chatto and Windus, 2019).

Bever, Edward, *The Realities of Witchcraft and Popular Magic in Early Modern Europe: Culture, Cognition and Everyday Life* (London: Palgrave, 2008).

Bickers, Robert, Tim Cole, Marianna Dudley, et al., 'Creative Dislocation: An Experiment in Collaborative Historical Research', *History Workshop Journal* 90:1 (2020), 273–96.

Blécourt, Willem de and Owen Davies (eds.), *Witchcraft Continued: Popular Magic in Modern Europe* (Manchester: Manchester University Press, 2004).

Blythe, Alecky, 'Alecky Blythe', in Will Hammond and Dan Steward (eds.), *Verbatim, Verbatim: Contemporary Documentary Theatre* (London: Oberon, 2012), 77–102.

Bouteiller, Marcelle, *Sorciers et jeteurs de sorts* (Paris: Plon, 1958).

Bubandt, Nils, *The Empty Seashell: Witchcraft and Doubt on an Indonesian Island* (Ithaca, NY and London: Cornell University Press, 2014).

Caladrone, Marina and Maggie Lloyd-Williams, *Actions: The Actors' Thesaurus* (London: Nick Hern Books, 2004).

Carlson, Marvin, *The Haunted Stage: The Theatre As Memory Machine* (Ann Arbor: University of Michigan Press, 2003).

Certeau, Michel de, *The Writing of History*, trans. Tom Conley (New York: Columbia University Press, 1988).

Churchill, Caryl, *Escaped Alone* (London: Samuel French, 2020).

Clark, Roy Peter, 'The Line between Fact and Fiction', in Mark Kramer and Wendy Call (eds.), *Telling True Stories: A Nonfiction Writers' Guide from the Nieman Foundation at Harvard University* (New York: Plume, 2007), 164–9.

Clark, Stuart, *Thinking with Demons: The Idea of Witchcraft in Early Modern Europe* (Oxford: Oxford University Press, 1997).

Conroy, Colette, *Theatre and the Body* (Basingstoke: Palgrave Macmillan, 2010).

Coste Lewis, Robin, *Voyage of the Sable Venus and Other Poems* (New York: Knopf, 2020).

Craig-Martin, Michael, *On Being an Artist* (London: Art Books Publishing, 2015).

Crouch, Tim, *An Oak Tree* (London: Oberon Books, 2015).

Darnton, Robert, *The Great Cat Massacre and Other Episodes in French Cultural History* (New York: Vintage Books, 1985).

Davidson, Hillary, 'The Embodied Turn: Making and Remaking Dress As an Academic Practice', *Fashion Theory* 23:3 (2019), 329–62.

Davies, Owen, *Magic: A Very Short Introduction* (Oxford: Oxford University Press, 2012).

  'Researching Reverse Witch Trials in Nineteenth- and Early Twentieth-Century England', in Jonathan Barry, Owen Davies, and Cornelie Usborne (eds.), *Cultures of Witchcraft from the Middle Ages to the Present: Essays in Honour of Willem de Blécourt* (Cham: Palgrave Macmillan, 2018), 215–33.

  'Witchcraft Accusations in France, 1850-1990', in Willem de Blécourt and Owen Davies (eds.), *Witchcraft Continued: Popular Magic in Modern Europe* (Manchester: Manchester University Press, 2004), 107–32.

  Witchcraft, Magic, and Culture, 1736–1951 (Manchester: Manchester University Press, 1999).

Davis, Natalie Zemon, *A Passion for History: Conversations with Denis Crouzet* (Kirksville, MO: Truman State University Press, 2010).

Deavere Smith, Anna and Carol Martin, 'The Word Becomes You: An Interview', *The Drama Review* 37:4 (1993), 45–62.

Devlin, Judith, *The Superstitious Mind: French Peasants and the Supernatural in the Nineteenth Century* (New Haven, CT: Yale University Press, 1987).

Dickinson, Emily, 'Tell All the Truth But Tell It Slant' [1951]. https://bit.ly/36jZby1.

Douglas, Mary, *Purity and Danger: An Analysis of Concepts of Pollution and Taboo* (London: Routledge, 1966).

Duden, Barbara, *The Woman beneath the Skin: A Doctor's Patients in Eighteenth-Century Germany*, trans. Thomas Dunlap (Cambridge, MA: Harvard University Press, 1991).

Favret-Saada, Jeanne, *The Anti-Witch*, trans. Matthew Carey (Hau Books: Chicago, 2009).

  Deadly Words: Witchcraft in the Bocage, trans. Catherine Cullen (Cambridge: Cambridge University Press, 1980).

  'Unbewitching as Therapy', *American Ethnologist* 16:1 (1989), 40–56.

Forsyth, Alison and Chris Megson, *Get Real: Documentary Theatre Past and Present* (Basingstoke: Palgrave Macmillan, 2009).

Freundschuh, Aaron, *The Courtesan and the Gigolo: The Murders in the Rue Montaigne and the Dark Side of Empire in Nineteenth-Century Paris* (Stanford, CA: Stanford University Press, 2017).

Geertz, Clifford, *The Interpretation of Cultures: Selected Essays* (New York: Basic Books, 2000).

Gennep, Arnold van, *Le folklore du Dauphiné (Isère)* (Paris: Librairie orientale et américaine, 1932).

Geschiere, Peter, *The Modernity of Witchcraft: Politics and the Occult in Postcolonial Africa* (Charlottesville: University Press of Virginia, 1997).

Gibson, Marion, *Reading Witchcraft: Stories of Early English Witches* (London and New York: Routledge, 1999).

Ginzburg, Carlo, *The Cheese and the Worms: The Cosmos of a Sixteenth-century Miller* (Baltimore, MD: Johns Hopkins University Press, 1992).

   The Night Battles: Witchcraft and Agrarian Cults in the Sixteenth and Seventeenth Centuries, trans. Anne Tedeschi and John Tedeschi (London: Routledge and Kegan Paul, 1983).

   Threads and Traces: True, False, Fictive (Berkeley: University of California Press, 2010).

Goldsmith, Kenneth, *Uncreative Writing: Managing Language in the Digital Age* (New York: Columbia University Press, 2011).

Gosden, Chris, *The History of Magic: From Alchemy to Witchcraft, from the Ice Age to the Present* (London: Viking, 2020).

Gowing, Laura, 'Secret Births and Infanticide in Seventeenth-Century England', *Past & Present* 156:1 (1997), 87–115.

Grafton, Anthony, *The Footnote: A Curious History* (Cambridge, MA: Harvard University Press, 1997).

Griffiths, Tom, *The Art of Time Travel: Historians and Their Craft* (Victoria: Schwartz Publishing, 2016).

Gustafsson, Laura and Terike Haapoja, *History according to Cattle* (Baltimore, MD: Project Muse, 2020).

Hammond, Will and Dan Steward, *Verbatim, Verbatim: Contemporary Documentary Theatre* (London: Oberon, 2012).

Haraway, Donna, *Staying with the Trouble: Making Kin in the Cthulucene* (Durham, NC: Duke University Press, 2016).

Hartman, Saidiya, *Wayward Lives, Beautiful Experiments: Intimate Histories of Riotous Black Girls, Troublesome Women, and Queer Radicals* (New York: W. W. Norton, 2019).

Hornby, Stephen, '"Stand Up if You're Gay!" *The Burnley Buggers' Ball*: The Dilemmas of Dramatizing Political History', Staging History Symposium, 26 April 2019, Bristol.

Houlbrook, Matt, *Prince of Tricksters: The Incredible True Story of Netley Lucas, Gentleman Crook* (Chicago, IL: University of Chicago Press, 2016).

Howe, Susan, *That This* (New York: New Directions, 2010).

Hughes, Ted, *Poetry in the Making: A Handbook for Writing* (London: Faber, 1969).

Hunter, Michael, *The Decline of Magic: Britain in the Enlightenment* (New Haven, CT: Yale University Press, 2020).

Hutton, Ronald, 'Anthropological and Historical Approaches to Witchcraft: Potential for a New Collaboration?' *The Historical Journal* 47:2 (2004), 413–34.

Jeffreys, Stephen, 'As a Playwright, You Must Have Something That You Want to Say', 2019. Nick Hern Books blog, https://bit.ly/34GeAIl.

Kara, Helen, *Creative Research Methods in the Social Sciences* (Bristol: Policy Press, 2015).

Kennedy, David and Christine Kennedy, *Women's Experimental Poetry in Britain, 1970–2010: Body, Time and Locale* (Liverpool: Liverpool University Press, 2013).

Mallarmé, Stéphane, 'Un coup de dés jamais n'abolira le hasard'. https://bit.ly/3Jag391.

Klinkenborg, Verlyn, *Several Short Sentences about Writing* (New York: Vintage Books, 2013).

Knott, Sarah, *Mother: An Unconventional History* (London: Penguin, 2019).

Krampl, Ulrike, *Les secrets des faux sorciers: Police, magie et escroquerie à Paris au XVIIIe siècle* (Paris: EHESS, 2012).

Lasky, Dorothea, Dominic Luxford, and Jesse Nathan, *Open the Door: How to Excite Young People about Poetry* (San Francisco, CA: McSweeney's, 2013).

Latour, Bruno, *On the Modern Cult of the Factish Gods* (Durham, NC: Duke University Press, 2010).

Lecoq, Jacques, *The Moving Body: Teaching Creative Theatre*, trans. David Bradby (London: Methuen Drama, 2002).

Lindsey, Kiera, *The Convict's Daughter: The Scandal that Shocked a Colony* (Crow's Nest, NSW: Allen and Unwin, 2016).

Liu, Tessie, 'Le Patrimoine Magique: Reassessing the Power of Women in Peasant Households in Nineteenth-Century France', *Gender and History* 6:1 (1994), 13–36.

Lowe, Hannah *Ormonde* (London: Hercules Editions, 2014).

Maiklem, Lara, *Mudlarking: Lost and Found on the River Thames* (London: Bloomsbury, 2019).

Mantel, Hilary, 'Can These Bones Live?' *The Reith Lectures*, 2017. https://bit .ly/3wuAV77.

'The Day is for the Living', *The Reith Lectures*, 2017. https://bit.ly/3Ixgau6.

'The Iron Maiden', *The Reith Lectures*, 2017. https://bit.ly/3JCQTQn.

Martin, Carol, *Theatre of the Real* (Basingstoke: Palgrave Macmillan, 2015).

Mason, Laura, 'The "Bosom of Proof": Criminal Justice and the Renewal of Oral Culture during the French Revolution', *The Journal of Modern History* 76:1 (2004), 29–61.

Miller, Brenda and Suzanne Paola, *Tell It Slant: Creating, Refining and Publishing Creative Nonfiction* (New York: McGraw-Hill, 2019).

Mol, Annemarie, *The Body Multiple: Ontology in Medical Practice* (Durham, NC: Duke University Press, 2002).

Morrison, Yedda, *Darkness* (Los Angeles, CA: Make Now Press, 2012).

Muir, Edward, 'Observing Trifles', in Edward Muir and Guido Ruggieri (eds.), *Microhistory and the Lost Peoples of Europe* (Baltimore, MD: Johns Hopkins University Press, 1991), vii–xviii.

Noguchi, Yone, 'A Proposal to American Poets', *The Reader* 3:3 (1904), 248.

NourbeSe Philip, M. and Setaey Adamu Boateng, *Zong!* (Middletown, CT: Wesleyan University Press, 2011).

O'Gorman, Emily and Andrea Gaynor, 'More-Than-Human Histories', *Environmental History* 25:4 (2020), 711–35.

Oliver, Mary, *A Poetry Handbook* (San Diego, CA: Harcourt Brace and Company, 1994).

Openstorytellers, the Company of, Nicola Grove, Simon Jarrett, et al., 'The Fortunes and Misfortunes of Fanny Fust', in Andrew W. M. Smith (ed.), *Paper Trails: The Social Life of Archives and Collections* (London: UCL Press, forthcoming).

Plunkett, Adam, 'Talk to the Dead: An Interview with Alice Notley', 2015. www.poetryfoundation.org/articles/70222/talk-to-the-dead.

Pooley, William G., 'Can the "Peasant" Speak? Witchcraft and Silence in Guillaume Cazaux's "The Mass of Saint-Sécaire', *Western Folklore* 71:2 (2012), 93–118.

'Magical Capital: Witchcraft and the Press in Paris, c.1789-1939', in Karl Bell (ed.), *Supernatural Cities: Enchantment, Anxiety and Spectrality* (Woodbridge, Suffolk: Boydell Press, 2019), 25–44.

Poynton, Robert, *Do Improvise: Less Push. More Pause. Better Results. A New Approach to Work (and Life)* (London: The Do Book Company, 2013).

Purkiss, Diane, *The Witch in History: Early Modern and Twentieth-Century Representations* (New York and London: Routledge, 1996).

Purpura, Lia, 'On Miniatures'. https://bit.ly/36kl94e.

Leopold von Ranke, 'Preface: Histories of Romance and Germanic Peoples', in Fritz Stern (ed.), *The Varieties of History: From Voltaire to the Present* (London: Macmillan, 1970).

Reinelt, Janelle, 'The Promise of Documentary', in Alison Forsyth and Chris Megson (eds.), *Get Real: Documentary Theatre Past and Present* (London: Palgrave Macmillan, 2009), 6–23.

Richardson, Laurel and Elizabeth Adams St Pierre, 'Writing: A Method of Inquiry', in Norman Denzin and Yvonna Lincoln (eds.), *Handbook of Qualitative Research* (London: Sage, 2000), 818–38.

Rokem, Freddie, *Performing History: Theatrical Representations of the Past in Contemporary Theatre* (Iowa City: Iowa University Press, 2000).

Roper, Lyndal, *Oedipus and the Devil: Witchcraft, Sexuality, and Religion in Early Modern Europe* (New York and London: Routledge, 1994).

Rublack, Ulinka, 'Fluxes: The Early Modern Body and Emotions', *History Workshop Journal* 53:1 (2002), 1–16.

Ruefle, Mary, 'On Erasure', in *Quarter After Eight* 16 (n.d). www.ohio.edu/cas/quarter-after-eight/table-contents#on.

Schneider, Rebecca, *Performing Remains: Art and War in Times of Theatrical Reenactment* (London: Routledge, 2011).

Segalen, Martine, *Love and Power in the Peasant Family: Rural France in the Nineteenth Century*, trans. Sarah Matthews (London: Blackwell, 1983).

Shaw, Clare, 'Gastromancy: Speaking from the Gut', 2016. https://poetryschool.com/theblog/gastromancy-speaking-gut/.

Shields, David, *Reality Hunger: A Manifesto* (New York: Knopf, 2010).

Shin, Sarah and Rebecca Tamás (eds.), *Spells: 21st-century Occult Poetry* (Newcastle: Ignota, 2018).

Singer, Ruth, *Criminal Quilts: Textiles Inspired by the Stories of Women Photographed in Stafford Prison 1877–1916* (Leicester: Independent Publishing Network, 2018).

Smith, Tracy K, 'Declaration', 2018. https://bit.ly/3JAgIk3.

Smyth, Cherry, *Famished* (Glasgow: Pindrop Press, 2019).

Sneddon, Andrew and John Fulton, 'Witchcraft, the Press, and Crime in Ireland, 1822-1922', *The Historical Journal* 62:3 (2019), 741–64.

Stoler, Ann Laura, *Along the Archival Grain: Epistemic Anxieties and Colonial Common Sense* (Princeton, NJ: Princeton University Press, 2009).

Strange, Julie-Marie, 'Reading Language as a Historical Source', in Simon Gunn and Lucy Faire (eds.), *Research Methods for History* (Edinburgh: Edinburgh University Press, 2016), 193–209.

Szijártó, István M. and Sigurður Gylfi Magnússon, *What is Microhistory? Theory and Practice* (London and New York: Routledge, 2013).

Talese, Gay, 'Delving into Private Lives', in Mark Kramer and Wendy Call (eds.), *Telling True Stories: A Nonfiction Writer's Guide from the Nieman Foundation at Harvard University* (New York: Plume, 2007), 6–9.

Tamás, Rebecca, 'Songs of Hecate', *The White Review* 24 (2019), https://bit.ly/3tKjQV6.

Taylor, Diana, *The Archive and the Repertoire: Performing Cultural Memory in the Americas* (Durham, NC: Duke University Press, 2003).

Trouillot, Michel-Rolph, *Silencing the Past: Power and the Production of History* (Boston, MA: Beacon Press, 1995).

Vuong, Ocean, 'How I Did It: Forward First Collection Special – Ocean Vuong on "Seventh Circle of Earth"'. https://bit.ly/3D0MZ1j.

Waters, Thomas. *Cursed Britain: A History of Witchcraft and Black Magic in Modern Times* (New Haven, CT: Yale University Press, 2019).

Cambridge Elements

Magic

Marion Gibson
University of Exeter

Marion Gibson is Professor of Renaissance and Magical Literatures and Director of the Flexible Combined Honours Programme at the University of Exeter. Her publications include *Possession, Puritanism and Print: Darrell, Harsnett, Shakespeare and the Elizabethan Exorcism Controversy* (2006), *Witchcraft Myths in American Culture* (2007), *Imagining the Pagan Past: Gods and Goddesses in Literature and History since the Dark Ages* (2013), *The Arden Shakespeare Dictionary of Shakespeare's Demonology* (with Jo Esra, 2014), *Rediscovering Renaissance Witchcraft* (2017) and *Witchcraft: The Basics* (2018). Her new book, *The Witches of St Osyth: Persecution, Murder and Betrayal in Elizabethan England*, will be published by CUP in 2022.

About the Series

Elements in Magic aims to restore the study of magic, broadly defined, to a central place within culture: one which it occupied for many centuries before being set apart by changing discourses of rationality and meaning. Understood as a continuing and potent force within global civilisation, magical thinking is imaginatively approached here as a cluster of activities, attitudes, beliefs and motivations which include topics such as alchemy, astrology, divination, exorcism, the fantastical, folklore, haunting, supernatural creatures, necromancy, ritual, spirit possession and witchcraft.

Cambridge Elements $\equiv$

Magic

Printed in the United States
by Baker & Taylor Publisher Services